PREHISTORIC, ROMAN MEDIEVAL OCCUPATION IN THE FROME VALLEY, GLOUCESTERSHIRE

edited by Martin Watts

A BEAKER PIT AND ROMANO-BRITISH SETTLEMENT AT FOXES FIELD, EBLEY ROAD, STONEHOUSE: EXCAVATIONS IN 2010–2011

by Mark Brett

MEDIEVAL ENCLOSURES AND A FISHPOND AT RECTORY MEADOWS, KINGS STANLEY: EXCAVATIONS IN 2011

by Alan Hardy and Jamie Wright

25 Years of Cotswold Archaeology

Bristol and Gloucestershire Archaeological Report No. 8

By agreement with Cotswold Archaeology this report is distributed free
to members of the Bristol and Gloucestershire Archaeological Society
To accompany Volume 131 of the Society's *Transactions* for 2013

Cotswold Archaeology Bristol and Gloucestershire Archaeological Report No. 8

Published by Cotswold Archaeology
© Authors and Cotswold Archaeology Ltd, 2013
Building 11, Kemble Enterprise Park, Cirencester, Gloucestershire GL7 6BQ

ISSN 1479-2389
ISBN 978-0-9553534-5-1

Cotswold Archaeology BAGAR series

1   **A Romano-British and Medieval Settlement Site at Stoke Road, Bishop's Cleeve, Gloucestershire**, by Dawn Enright and Martin Watts, 2002

2   **Later Prehistoric and Romano-British Burial and Settlement at Hucclecote, Gloucestershire**, by Alan Thomas, Neil Holbrook and Clifford Bateman, 2003

3   **Twenty-Five Years of Archaeology in Gloucestershire: a review of new discoveries and new thinking in Gloucestershire, South Gloucestershire and Bristol, 1979–2004**, edited by Neil Holbrook and John Juřica, 2006

4   **Two Cemeteries from Bristol's Northern Suburbs**, edited by Martin Watts, 2006

5   **Prehistoric and Medieval Occupation at Moreton-in-Marsh and Bishop's Cleeve, Gloucestershire**, edited by Martin Watts, 2007

6   **Iron Age and Romano-British Agriculture in the North Gloucestershire Severn Vale**, edited by Neil Holbrook, 2008

7   **Medieval and Post-Medieval Development within Bristol's Inner Suburbs**, edited by Martin Watts, 2011

8   **Prehistoric, Romano-British and Medieval Occupation in the Frome Valley, Gloucestershire**, edited by Martin Watts, 2013

Cover image: Romano-British quern stone from Foxes Field, Ebley Road, Stonehouse. Photograph by Adam Stanford © Aerial-Cam Ltd / Cotswold Archaeology.

Series Editor: Martin Watts
Produced by Past Historic, Kings Stanley, Gloucestershire, GL10 3HW
Printed in Great Britain by Henry Ling Limited, Dorchester, DT1 1HD

FOREWORD

As Cotswold Archaeology enters its 25th year I am pleased to present our eighth *Bristol and Gloucestershire Archaeological Report*, which describes the results of two excavations in the Frome valley, at Stonehouse and Kings Stanley. There is little to connect the two sites, other than them being less than a mile apart, with the site at Foxes Field, Stonehouse, principally comprising an early Roman-British rural settlement and late Romano-British burial ground; and the site at Rectory Meadows, Kings Stanley, featuring medieval paddocks and a late medieval pond. In fact, with Foxes Field also producing evidence for prehistoric occupation and for a post-medieval path and plough furrows, the two sites largely complement each other in terms of period representation. However, common to both sites is evidence, of just a few fragments of flue tiles, roof tiles and building rubble, to suggest that late Roman villas once stood nearby to both locations. It is the recurring presence of Romano-British remains from archaeological investigations in the Frome valley, often with such evidence for high-status buildings, which demonstrates just how populated this area was during the Roman period in Britain. The burials from Foxes Field, and in particular the close bond that can be implied between the man and woman found in the remarkable 'double' grave, serve to remind us that these discoveries are not just 'relics of a bygone age', but were once homes to real people who lived, loved and died beside the river Frome.

Cotswold Archaeology has come a long way in 25 years. From our relatively humble origins in 1989 as Cotswold Archaeological Trust, the successor body to the Cirencester Excavation Committee, we have grown to become one of the largest providers of archaeological services in the country, currently with a staff of around 100, an annual turnover in excess of £5 million, and a nationwide operation from offices now firmly established in Milton Keynes and Andover to complement the geographic coverage possible from Cirencester.

This report series, produced at Cotswold Archaeology's own expense to accompany the *Transactions of the Bristol and Gloucestershire Archaeological Society*, represents our ongoing commitment to the timely publication of our work and its dissemination to as wide an audience as possible. Yet formal publication represents only a part of the archaeological work we undertake: a great deal of valuable archaeological knowledge has, hitherto, remained relatively inaccessible within unpublished 'grey literature' reports produced as part of the planning process. As part of our 25 years' celebrations, in 2014 we will launch our *Archaeological Reports Online* website facility (at www.cotswoldarchaeology.co.uk), providing easy and free access to well over 2000 of our 'grey literature' reports, as well as signposting the way to our formal publications that are also now available online. We believe this will be a fitting way to mark our 25th anniversary, and we look forward to the next 25 years of archaeological investigation and discovery with confidence and excitement.

Martin Watts
Head of Publications, Cotswold Archaeology
January 2014

CONTENTS

Foxes Field, Ebley Road, Stonehouse

Rectory Meadows, Kings Stanley

ABSTRACTS

Foxes Field, Ebley Road, Stonehouse: Excavations in 2010–2011

Excavations at Foxes Field revealed evidence for prehistoric and Romano-British occupation, as well as for later ridge-and-furrow cultivation and a post-medieval lane. Mesolithic and Neolithic activity was represented by residual flints only, but an assemblage of Beaker pottery and flints from a three-throw pit indicated transient settlement at the site in the late 3rd millennium BC. A few pits and postholes from the 1st century BC or early 1st century AD suggested small-scale activity in the Later Iron Age, which was followed by a major period of settlement and use of the site throughout the Roman period, from the later 1st century AD to the 4th century AD. An enclosure was constructed in the early Roman period, with a trackway leading northwards. Evidence for activity was concentrated within the enclosure and included the remains of possible oven bases and a drying oven, as well as two middens and numerous pits and postholes. Metalworking waste from smelting and smithing was recovered from some of these features. In the later Roman period (3rd to 4th centuries AD), the site was used for burial, with 14 graves excavated from the area of the enclosure. The vast majority of burials were of adults, and included one grave with a male and female closely flexed together. The evidence suggests that the main locus of settlement lay beyond the limits of excavation to the south of the site, and there was artefactual evidence to suggest that a villa house may have formed part of this settlement by the 3rd or 4th century AD.

Rectory Meadows, Kings Stanley: Excavations in 2011

Excavations at Rectory Meadows revealed a sequence of small enclosures dating to the 11th to 13th centuries, possibly part of a settlement pre-dating the borough established in the south of the parish in the mid 13th century. The subsequent construction of a large fishpond in the late 13th or 14th century may have been associated with the newly established Rectory, although it was infilled well before the Rectory's earliest known documentary reference. A small quantity of residual Roman finds suggests that there was a nearby settlement dating to the 2nd to 4th century AD, distinct from the Roman settlement known to have existed at the northern end of Kings Stanley, near the manor and church.

A BEAKER PIT AND ROMANO-BRITISH SETTLEMENT AT FOXES FIELD, EBLEY ROAD, STONEHOUSE: EXCAVATIONS IN 2010–2011

by Mark Brett

with contributions by
Sarah Cobain, Jonny Geber, Neil Holbrook, E.R. McSloy,
Sarah Paynter and Fiona Roe

INTRODUCTION

This report presents the results of excavations carried out by Cotswold Archaeology between September 2010 and March 2011 at Foxes Field, Ebley Road, Stonehouse (centred on NGR: SO 82080478; Fig. 1). The work was undertaken at the request of Barratt Homes (Bristol) as a condition of Planning Consent for residential development. The excavation was undertaken in accordance with a brief prepared by Charles Parry, Senior Archaeological Officer, Gloucestershire County Council (archaeological advisors to the local planning authority, Stroud District Council), who also monitored both the fieldwork and the post-excavation analysis.

Site location, geology and topography

The site is approximately 1.2km to the east of Stonehouse on the northern side of Ebley Road, the Stonehouse to Ebley section of the B4008. Covering an area of *c.* 3ha, it is bounded to the north by the Gloucester to Swindon railway, with residential development to the east and west. Located *c.* 200m to the north of the Frome, the ground rises gently to the north from *c.* 40m to 50m AOD (Fig. 2). The underlying solid geology of the area is mapped as Pleistocene third terrace gravels of the River Frome (BGS 1975). However, lias clay was encountered throughout the site, with bands of gravel occurring only within its easternmost extent.

Archaeological Background

To inform the planning authority of the archaeological potential of the area, a desk-based assessment (Etheridge 2008), geophysical survey (GeoQuest 2009) and field evaluation (Young 2009a) were carried out. The assessment identified cropmarks visible on aerial photographs (NMR 216; 1102; 9399; 10196), which suggested that medieval furrows and a curvilinear feature lay within the proposed development area. The evaluation confirmed the presence of furrow cultivation, but did not find a feature corresponding to the cropmark. However, it also indicated that some of the magnetic anomalies plotted by geophysical survey related to a previously unknown Romano-British settlement and found additional evidence for prehistoric activity. As a consequence, a condition was attached to the planning permission that required excavation in advance of development. Prior to development, the site comprised a single arable field with previous use as a market garden.

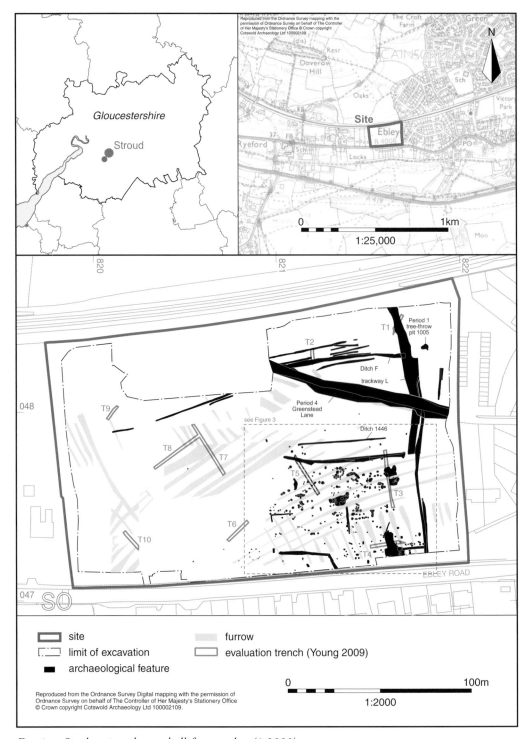

Fig. 1   Site location plan and all-feature plan (1:2000)

Fig. 2   The site, looking south across Ebley Road and the Frome valley

Excavation methodology

Excavation commenced with the removal of topsoil by mechanical excavator. The underlying archaeological features were hand-excavated according to a strategy approved by Charles Parry. The methodology adopted was for the excavation a minimum of 20% of all linear features (unless a smaller sample provided adequate proof of date), at least 50% of all discrete features, and 100% excavation of highly significant features (e.g. funerary, ritual, domestic or industrial).

EXCAVATION RESULTS

An area of approximately 2.4ha was excavated. Archaeological features were found throughout this area but with the vast majority concentrated within the south-eastern quarter (Fig. 3). Stratigraphic analysis, combined with the artefactual evidence indicated that four main periods of activity were represented:

Period 1: Late Neolithic/Early Bronze Age (late 3rd millennium BC)
Period 2: Late Iron Age to Early Roman (1st century BC to 1st century AD)
Period 3: Roman (late 1st to 4th century AD)
Period 4: medieval to modern (11th to 19th century)

The deep furrows of medieval ridge-and-furrow cultivation and modern ploughing had significantly truncated many of these features, and there was also evidence of root disturbance and animal burrowing, probably attributable to the former use of the site as a market garden.

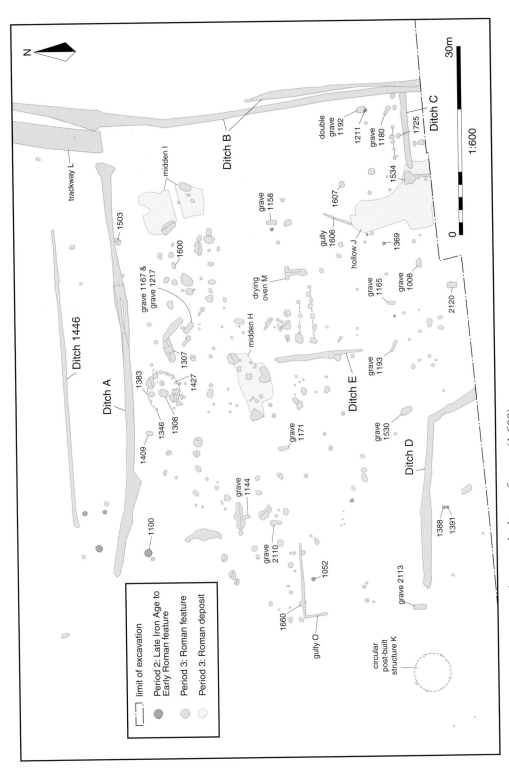

Fig. 3   Plan of the Roman enclosure and adjacent features (1:600)

Period 1: Late Neolithic/Early Bronze Age (late 3rd millennium BC)

Tree-throw pit 1005, in the north-eastern corner of the site (Fig. 1), was an irregular oval shape in plan, with gently sloping sides except along the south-western extent. It contained two fills, the earlier of which comprised displaced natural clay, presumably dragged up by the roots of the tree when it fell. The later fill, thought to represent backfilling of the feature, contained 57 sherds of Beaker pottery, originating from at least eight individual vessels, together with a group of 18 worked flints. Two distinctive end-scrapers indicate that the lithics from this feature are probably contemporary with the recovered pottery.

Further prehistoric flints, of which ten were worked, were recovered as residual finds from later features. These included a Mesolithic adze and microlith, and a broken leaf-shaped arrowhead of early Neolithic date. The bulk of the remaining residual lithics comprised debitage which is most likely broadly dated to the later Neolithic or Bronze Age periods.

Period 2: Late Iron Age to Early Roman (1st century BC to 1st century AD)

The handmade late Iron Age/transitional pottery types that were found within the features of this period have a date range that spans the Late Iron Age to Early Roman periods. Featured sherds suggest this range can be refined to between the 1st century BC and later 1st century AD. A small number of pits and postholes that contained this pottery possibly pre-dated the Roman Conquest, whilst in other features this transitional pottery was mixed with early forms of Roman pottery.

The Period 2 pits and postholes were found amongst the later Roman activity within the south-eastern quadrant of the site (Fig. 3). Pit 1100 was of particular note amongst a small cluster of four pits around the western terminus of (later) Ditch A. This pit contained a series of fills (Fig. 4), including charcoal-rich deposit 1101 and a fill containing 2.8kg of fired-clay fragments which exhibit clear wattle impressions and curving external surfaces, perhaps representing the remains of a domed oven. A total of 250 sherds of pottery, including 238 sherds from the same contexts as the fired clay, was recovered from this feature, accounting for 18.5% of the assemblage of Late Iron Age/transitional-type pottery from the entire site. Two environmental samples taken from pit 1100 contained crop-processing plant remains dominated by spelt wheat. This material may have been

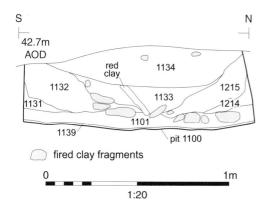

Fig. 4   Period 2 (Late Iron Age/Early Roman) pit 1100: in section (1:20) and looking west, scale 0.4m

redeposited from one of the three pits that exhibited *in situ* scorching, located along the southern edge of Period 3 Ditch A. These are discussed within Period 3 on the basis of two sherds of Roman pottery relating to a secondary use of one of these pits, but it may be that these are further evidence of activity in Period 2.

Three pits located towards the southern periphery of the site contained the severely truncated remains of single vessels of handmade Late Iron Age/transitional pottery, which appeared to have been set upright within them. Pits 1388 and 1391 were found in close proximity, to the south of later Roman Ditch D, while pit 1369 was located on the western edge of the later Roman hollow J. The pits were circular, with diameters of between 0.35m and 0.45m and a maximum depth of 0.25m, and they were just large enough to hold the vessels within them, suggesting that they had been dug specifically for that purpose. Sherds of mid 1st-century AD date within the backfill of pit 1388 suggest that this feature, and by association pits 1369 and 1391, belong to this period. The pots may have been a form of cold storage. It seems unlikely that they once contained cremated burials as micro-excavation of the fills of the three vessels identified no bone, organic remains or residues, and no residual cremated bone was found anywhere on site. The remainder of the features from which only handmade transitional pottery was found comprise three widely distributed pits, and posthole 1211. Of these features, pit 1052 lay close to undated L-shaped gully O, ascribed to Period 3 but which may alternatively belong here.

Period 3: Roman (late 1st to 4th century AD) (Figs 1 and 3)

The majority of the features excavated belonged to this period. An area partially enclosed by three ditches (A, B and C/D) in the south-eastern part of the site contained a concentration of features including a stone-built drying oven, three areas of finds-rich midden deposits, another ditch, two gullies, and over 300 other features comprising mainly pits and postholes, but also including 14 burials (Fig. 3). A trackway (L) ran northwards from the north-east corner of this enclosure, and a small number of features were also found to the north, south and west of the enclosed area. Dating evidence for this period covers a wide span within the Roman period. Given the broad date ranges of some of the Roman pottery, the high levels of residuality within some features and the damage to upper fills by later agricultural activity, it was difficult to distinguish any phases within this period with any certainty; however, it is possible to suggest that the enclosure and the trackway were established early on in this period, and that the burials date to after the enclosure had been (largely) abandoned. The bulk of the pottery spans the late 1st to 2nd centuries AD, suggesting the enclosure was mainly in use during that period. The date of a small amount of pottery from midden I, in the north-western part of the enclosure, extends into the 3rd century AD, whilst that from the hollow J and a single pit at the southern limit of the excavation suggest a shift in activity to the south in the 3rd to 4th century AD. The Late Roman pottery associated with the drying oven probably reflects its date of demolition rather than of its use.

The enclosure
Ditches A and B appeared to define the north and east sides of a rectilinear enclosure, approximately 75m long and 50m wide, within which the majority of archaeological features were contained. Ditches C and D formed a discontinuous boundary on the south

side of the enclosure and may represent internal divisions within a larger enclosure; Ditch D turned to the south-east and continued beyond the limit of excavation. There was no evidence for a western boundary to the enclosure and it is assumed that it was open on this side, or bounded by a less substantial feature such as a fence, bank or hedge, for which no evidence survived. There was no evidence of bank material adjacent to any of the ditches, and the presence of cut features close to the ditches suggests that, if banks were originally present, they did not survive for long.

The construction of the enclosure may have taken place in the latter part of the 1st century AD, with Late Iron Age/transitional pottery well represented in the material recovered from the primary fills of Ditches B and D, mixed with early types of Roman pottery. Slightly later dating, into the 2nd century AD, may be suggested for Ditches A and C, but this may be a result of later re-cutting, which was in evidence along Ditch A in particular.

Ditch A comprised a number of intercutting lengths, giving a total length of 65m. It was aligned east/west and was up to 1.8m wide and 0.75m deep. The earliest ditch fills appeared to be a result of both silting and infilling, including dumps of settlement debris. Large quantities of pottery indicated deposition continued well into the 2nd century AD. There were also small quantities of animal bone, ceramic building material, fired clay and slag. The final recut of Ditch A was filled with settlement debris, including quantities of animal bone, slag, fired clay, ceramic building material, daub, burnt stone, worked flint and iron objects, together with 947 sherds of pottery dating predominately to the mid to late 2nd century AD. A large proportion of the finds, including 598 sherds of pottery, was recovered from the deep, bulbous re-cut eastern terminus. Most notable was a copper-alloy finger ring, complete with opaque blue glass setting (Fig.10, no. 6).

Forming the eastern boundary to the enclosure, Ditch B was slightly sinuous and survived to a maximum width of 1.6m and a depth of 0.4m. The ditch had mainly silted up but there was also some evidence for infilling, from which small quantities of pottery from the mid-1st to mid-3rd century AD was recovered. The southern part of the ditch had been recut just to the east, from which 143 sherds of mid to late 1st to 2nd-century AD pottery were recovered. Small quantities of animal bone, fired clay and residual worked flint were also found. Ditch B continued beyond the southern limit of the site, and ran beyond the enclosure to the north where it had been eroded away by trackway L (Fig. 1).

Ditch C, which formed the south-east corner of the enclosure with Ditch B, was up to 1.2m wide and 0.25m deep. It yielded a small amount of finds, including a few sherds of pottery from the mid-1st to mid-3rd-century AD. Its relationship with hollow J to the west was obscured by a later furrow. Ditch D was up to 1.75m wide and 0.6m deep, and contained up to four separate fills, including localised slumping soon after construction and a period of silting up before the ditch had been infilled. No evidence of re-cutting was identified. The recovery of nearly 500 sherds of pottery, almost exclusively dated to the mid to late 1st to early 2nd century AD, suggests the disposal of domestic refuse in the ditch. Other finds included quantities of animal bone; fired clay; residual worked flint; a naturally perforated stone that may have been used as a loomweight; fragments of copper-alloy strips and a copper-alloy brooch of Polden Hill type.

A further ditch, E, was found in the centre of the enclosure on a parallel alignment to Ditch B. Ditch E was 14m long and up to 1m wide, and tapered away to the south. It contained a single fill which included pottery dated to the mid to late 1st to 3rd century AD. The function that this ditch served is unclear.

1st to 2nd-century AD features within the enclosure

The vast majority of features within the enclosure comprised discrete pits and postholes, all containing very similar, dark silty clay fills, presumably derived from the contemporary topsoil. Most contained late 1st to 2nd-century AD pottery.

At the presumed western limit of the enclosure, L-shaped gully O, which measured approximately 16m in total length, was sharp cornered and may have represented a drip gully associated with a rectangular building in timber or cob, which otherwise left no trace. Gully O was filled with homogeneous silts. Although essentially undated it was cut by pit 1660, part of a small band of pits and postholes of Roman date to the north of this gully.

Three pits (1383, 1409 and 1503) close to the southern edge of Ditch A exhibited evidence for *in situ* burning (or having had heated material deposited within them) and may have been the bases of ovens used for domestic or small-scale industrial activity within this part of the site. Pit 1383 was oval in shape, 1.2m long and 0.88m wide. Although it was relatively shallow, the underlying natural clay was scorched to a depth of 0.2m, indicating a high firing temperature. The fill of the pit comprised hard-baked clay containing no finds. To the west of pit 1383, pit 1409 was of similar shape and size in plan. The natural substrate at the base of this feature had been scorched to a depth of 0.07m. The pit contained three fills, the earliest of which contained fragments of fired clay, possibly from a collapsed superstructure. This was covered by a fill derived from natural silting, which was in turn sealed by a charcoal-rich deposit suggesting re-use of the partially infilled pit. Two sherds of pottery of broadly Roman date were recovered from the second fill of the pit. To the east, square pit 1503 was the smallest of the three pits exhibiting evidence for *in situ* burning, again with the evidence for a heat-affected clay lining, but it was devoid of finds. Environmental samples from each of the three pits contained no evidence to suggest what processes they were associated with. It is possible that these pits were associated with Late Iron Age pit 1100 (Period 2, above) which yielded evidence for crop processing.

Pit 1383 lay on the edge of a possible semi-circular post-built structure approximately 5m in diameter, although its proximity to the structure suggests it was not contemporary. Posthole 1346 of the possible post-built structure contained redeposited burnt material, as did pits 1308 and 1427. To the east of this, and possibly also associated with this activity, was L-shaped trench 1307, measuring approximately 6m in total length, up to 1.10m wide and up to 0.15m deep. This trench could have been the foundation for an associated structure, although its mixed sandy clay and rubble fill suggested that it had been robbed out, and some of the rubble fill was burnt.

The vast majority of the pits and postholes within the enclosure were unremarkable in their size, shape or content. A number of larger pits and a few of the postholes contained post packing, and post-pipes were also visible, but no coherent building plans were evident. Two rows of postholes to the west of drying oven M (below) were too close together to have been for the walls of a building, but may represent fencelines or a rack. An alignment of postholes was along the northern side of Ditch C may represent the line of another fence.

Two irregularly shaped deposits of dark, silty clay material represent the remains of middens, covering areas of 11m by 5.1m (midden H) and 10.5m by 6.95m (midden I). Both survived within shallow hollows to a maximum depth of 0.12m. They are likely to have been significantly larger originally, but had been subject to considerable truncation by later furrows and subsequent mechanical ploughing. Whilst both contained quantities of plant remains, more artefacts were recovered from midden H than midden I, including 229 sherds of 2nd-century AD pottery. The eight sherds from midden I also dated to the 2nd century AD. Excavation of midden I revealed underlying pits, a posthole and seven stakeholes, some containing pottery types that continued into the 3rd century AD. The fills of these features were similar to the midden and the relationships between them were not generally discernible. The features beneath midden H included large pits, as well as three probable tree-throw pits. Generally, these contained small quantities of pottery of late 1st to 2nd-century AD date, animal bone and ceramic building material. A copper-alloy nail cleaner was recovered from one pit (Fig. 10, no. 4).

Later features in the area of the enclosure

A drying oven (M), located close to the centre of the enclosure, was 'T'-shaped in plan and constructed from rough limestone blocks bonded with clay (Fig. 5). It was 3.3m long, 1.8m wide at its widest extent and up to 0.2m in height, with a maximum of two courses of surviving stonework. The internal flue passage was 0.5m wide, lined with a thin layer of charcoal-rich silt, thickening towards the southern opening although no evidence for a stoking pit survived. A sample of this material contained cereal remains dominated by spelt wheat (indicative of crop processing) as well as large amounts of fired-clay fragments, probably from a collapsed superstructure. This layer was sealed by rubble, presumably from the demolition of the remainder of the structure, from which a few sherds of 3rd to 4th-century AD pottery were recovered.

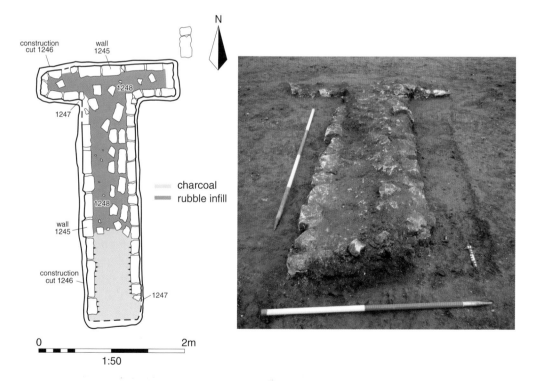

Fig. 5   Period 3 (Roman) drying oven: in plan (1:40) and looking north, scales 2m and 1m

In the south-eastern corner of the site, a similar deposit to that found in middens H and I filled hollow J (Fig. 3), which extended for a distance of 14m into the site and gradually deepened and widened to the south, to a maximum width of 11m and depth of 0.35m at the limit of excavation. This feature may represent the infilled northern end of a hollowed trackway, similar to trackway L to the north, possibly a depression created by livestock passing through a gateway. The infilling of the hollow was rich in finds including an abundance of burnt stone, fired clay, slag, worked flint and iron objects, including over 30 nails, as well as small quantities of animal bone and coal; the bulky material was probably chosen to consolidate the ground, an assumption supported by the well-broken pottery assemblage of over 600 sherds dated to the 3rd to 4th centuries AD. Amongst the artefacts of particular note were copper-alloy sheet fragments, possibly from mirrors; a coin dated to AD 353–4; a late 1st to 2nd-century AD bow brooch and a fragment of vessel glass. Iron objects included a holdfast and T-clamp, riveted strips, part of a knife and a probable padlock key. The ceramic building material included fragments of box-flue tile, *tegula* and brick. The 8.79kg of slag derived from smelting as well as smithing. Smithing and smelting waste was also found in pit 1534 (below hollow J) and pit 1725 to the east, but in all locations appeared to have been redeposited. A narrow gully (1606) ran into the northern end of hollow J, from which part of a decorated copper-alloy 'snake's-head' bracelet was recovered (Fig. 10, no. 5).

Adjacent to the southern limit of excavation, rectangular pit 2120 was 1.55m long, 0.8m wide and 0.55m deep, with vertically cut sides and a flat base. Its four very distinct fills contained some unusual finds that suggest intentional collection and deposition. The earliest fill comprised dark brown organic material from which a quantity of late 3rd to 4th-century AD pottery was recovered, along with a possible awl made from a red deer antler tine. Overlying this was deposited rubble and clay containing roof and box-flue tile, together with small quantities of other finds. This was sealed by a charcoal-rich layer and finally by a rubble deposit which contained a coin of AD 260–8, a curated silver Iron Age coin dated to *c.* 30–15 BC, and two fragments of quartz conglomerate quernstone. Only half of the smaller example was present; the larger stone retained a piece of the iron rynd cemented into the central hole and was almost complete (Fig. 11). Other finds comprised an iron shears blade, large quantities of animal bone and pottery.

The burials

A total of 14 human inhumations was excavated from within graves, and an additional inhumation was identified from disarticulated remains (for details see *Grave Catalogue*, below). All of the burials were within the area of the Roman enclosure, though grave 2113 lay just to the west of the terminus of Ditch D. The preservation of the skeletal remains varied, with some significantly truncated by medieval or later ploughing, although a number survived in relatively good condition. Pottery recovered from the backfills of the graves is likely to be residual, and cannot be used as a reliable indicator of the date of the burial, other than to supply a *terminus post quem*. From the dateable grave goods found in some burials and the evidence for certain burial practices, all the inhumations can be assigned to the later Roman period. Limited stratigraphic evidence was available, in that grave 1217, located towards the northern extent of the enclosure and with 2nd to 3rd-century AD pottery in its backfill, was cut by later grave 1167; and grave 1192, located within the south-eastern corner of the enclosure, cut Period 2 posthole 1211. There was no

Fig. 6   Period 3 (Roman) double burial Sk 1190 and Sk 1191 in grave 1192, looking west. Scales 1m and 0.4m

other evidence of intercutting between the burials and other features, except for truncation by furrows or other later cultivation features.

The inhumations included prone, supine, flexed, crouched and extended examples on a variety of orientations. Grave 1192 contained the skeletons of an older adult male and female, positioned together in a flexed position with the male behind the female (Fig. 6). There was no clear correlation between the distribution of graves and their burial attributes, orientation, age and/or sex, although all five male burials were towards the southern end of the enclosure, with three of them orientated SE-NW, and the other two orientated N-S (including the male in the double burial). The majority of the inhumations appeared to have been laid directly into the graves; however, there was evidence within three of the burials for the presence of wooden coffins, in the form of coffin nails.

The recovery of iron hobnails or shoe cleats around the feet of seven of the inhumations demonstrates that they were buried wearing footwear, a practice that became commonplace in burials associated with rural settlements during the late 2nd and 3rd centuries AD (Philpott 1991, 167), although they are also found in burials as late as the 6th–7th centuries AD. In grave 1193, the skeleton was prone, hobnails were recovered from the feet, and a coin dated to AD 324–30 was found adjacent to the mouth area. The custom of placing a coin in the mouth of an inhumation as the fare for the ferryman Charon for safe passage across the River Styx in the afterlife was commonplace by the 4th century (ibid., 214–5).

Other finds associated with the inhumations include a fragment of a lead vessel or sheet from grave 1217, a lead pot repair from grave 1180 and, perhaps most notably, a sizeable iron cleaver (Fig. 10, no.1) interred next to the female inhumation within grave 1171, to the west of midden H. This is an uncommon find from a grave, and most known examples date to the Late Roman period. A flint blade from grave 1158 was probably residual.

In addition to these burials, the partial remains of a neonatal skeleton were recovered from pit 1600, 5m to the west of midden I. This was the only neonate burial found on the site and the only human remains that were not formally interred.

Features external to the enclosure

The density of features to the north and west of the enclosure was considerably less than within it. A circular post-built structure (K) was revealed about 10m to the west of the terminus of Ditch D. It was *c.* 6m in diameter and comprised eight relatively small postholes, all containing charcoal, suggesting that the structure had been burnt *in situ*; one posthole contained 2nd-century AD pottery.

Approximately 9m to the north of Ditch A, Ditch 1446 was undated but its alignment suggests that it was also part of the Roman activity, and its silt fill suggested it had been a drainage ditch (Fig. 3). Some 50m to the north of the enclosure, Ditch F extended for 65m on an east/west alignment across the northern part of the site (Fig. 1). It survived to a width of between 0.7m and 2.1m and a depth of between 0.15m and 0.75m. It was cut at its most westerly exposed extent by the Period 4 remains of Greenstead Lane (below), and contained a single homogeneous silty clay fill from which a few finds of slag, pottery, residual worked flint and fragments of pennant sandstone roof tile were recovered. It may also have served as a drainage ditch. A series of broadly parallel narrow linear features, some intercutting, were revealed to either side of Ditch F. These were between 0.15m and 0.8m in width, and 0.05m and 0.3m in depth. These are difficult to interpret but they may represent Roman cultivation features. They contained a few finds that included a small quantity of Roman pottery. A discontinuous pair of narrow parallel features within the north-western part of the site probably represents similar activity.

A broad, shallow, slightly curving feature, L, extended from the north-eastern corner of the site southwards to the entrance at the north-eastern corner of the enclosure, cutting through Ditches B and F. This appears to represent a hollow-way up to 7.5m wide and 0.6m deep. The fill of this trackway, which appears to have derived from general silting, included a small number of pottery sherds broadly dated as Roman, as well as a group of nine worked flints recovered from one location towards the northern exposed extent of the feature.

Several pits and postholes to the south of Ditches C and D indicate that activity continued southwards beyond the limit of excavation, as did hollow J and Ditches B and D.

Period 4: medieval to 19th century (Fig. 1)

A co-axial pattern of furrows associated with ridge-and-furrow cultivation was observed throughout the site. These were aligned approximately north-east/south-west and north-west/south-east, and the intercutting furrows indicate that there were two phases of this activity. No medieval pottery was found, although this method of cultivation is typical of this period. A single sherd of post-medieval pottery was recovered from one of the furrows and others contained quantities of residual Roman finds.

A broad ridge of material mainly composed of stone, ceramic building material and ashy deposits crossed the north-eastern part of the site on an north-west/south-east alignment, post-dating all other features. This matched the alignment of Greenstead Lane, a trackway that divided land, belonging to Stonehouse parish to the south from Randwick parish to the north, on the Tithe Survey maps of 1839 (GRO/P316a SD2) and 1842 (GRO/GDR/T1/146). The lane may represent an earlier route between Ebley and Stonehouse, although only 19th-century material was found during excavation. The lane fell out of use after it was bisected by the railway line to the north of the site in 1845 (Etheridge 2008).

THE FINDS

Lithics, by E.R. McSloy

Lithics amounting to 179 pieces was recovered from 65 deposits. The group includes a small quantity of heat-affected (but not worked) material (Table 1). The bulk of material was hand recovered, with 16 pieces retrieved from bulk soil samples. The worked flint was scanned by context and fully recorded. Attributes recorded include type, count, colour and conditional aspects including patination/cortication and where 'rolled'.

The large bulk of the assemblage was clearly redeposited, recovered from late prehistoric and Roman dated features. A small group of 18 worked pieces and one burnt flint was recovered from tree-throw pit 1005, which also yielded Beaker-type pottery and which is the only feature assigned to Period 1 (Late Neolithic/Early Bronze Age).

Condition

The majority of the lithics had some degree of breakage or edge damage, although only a few pieces were excessively edge-damaged or 'rolled'. A significant proportion (75 pieces or 42%) was patinated, this varying from a light mottled discolouration to an overall white. The group from the Period 1 tree-throw pit was almost entirely heavily patinated; presumably the result of deposition over time in a calcareous burial environment. This Period 1 group was mainly 'sharp', and contained the small removals often associated with stratified groups.

Raw material comprises primarily mid or darker grey flint, with a few of pale grey, reddish brown and 'honey-coloured' examples. The quality appears to be good, with no instances of heavily flawed flint recorded. The surviving cortex is generally thick and unabraded, suggesting the use of chalk or chalk-soil sources. Several cores from the assemblage were worked down to a very small size (their average weight is only 34g), a factor consistent with an area where flint is not naturally present and where good quality material would be worked until unpractical.

Composition and Dating

Pieces with secondary working amount to only 13 items (7.3%), of which three pieces, all scrapers, came from the Period 1 tree-throw pit. Among the redeposited material there is evidence for activity across the Mesolithic, Early Neolithic and the Late Neolithic/Early Bronze Age.

Mesolithic activity is evidenced by single examples of an adze (Fig. 7, no. 1) and a microlith (Fig. 7, no. 2) and two backed blades. Single/opposed platform bladelet cores, rejuvenation flakes/keeled flakes and blades/bladelets also probably date to this period, as might a proportion of the scrapers and flake debitage. The adze is a rare example of this class from western counties.

Broken leaf arrowhead (Fig. 7, no. 4) is the only piece certainly of Early Neolithic date, although a proportion of the blades and flakes might also belong to this period. No dating can be ascribed with certainty to the scrapers, which account for the remainder of the

Table 1: Worked flint summary by type and period

Class	Artefacts type	1	2	3	4	Unph.	Total
Tools	arrowhead broken	-	-	1	-	-	1
	blade backed broken	-	-	1	-	-	1
	blade backed	-	-	-	1	-	1
	Microl. broken	-	-	1	-	-	1
	pick or adze	-	-	1	-	-	1
	scraper	-	-	2	-	-	2
	scraper broken	1	-	-	-	-	1
	scraper end	1	-	1	1	-	3
	scraper end broken	1	-	-	-	-	1
	scraper end/side broken	-	-	-	1	-	1
Sub-total		*3*	*-*	*7*	*3*	*-*	*13*
Debitage	blade	-	-	2	1	-	3
	blade broken	-	1	4	4	-	9
	blade utilised	-	-	-	1	-	1
	bladelet	-	-	2	5	-	7
	bladelet broken	-	-	6	5	-	11
	chip	-	-	18	2	2	22
	chip broken	-	-	2	1	-	3
	core	-	1	3	4	1	9
	core rejuve	-	-	1	-	-	1
	flake	9	-	30	17	2	58
	flake broken	5	2	19	4	-	30
	flake retouched	1	-	-	1	-	2
	keeled flake broken	-	-	2	-	-	2
	shatter	-	-	3	1	-	4
Sub-total		*15*	*4*	*92*	*46*	*5*	*162*
Burnt	(unworked)	1	-	3	-	-	4
	Totals	*19*	*4*	*102*	*49*	*5*	*179*

tools, although the examples from tree-throw pit 1005 are feasibly contemporary with the Beaker pottery.

Flakes/broken flakes and other debitage types make up the bulk of the assemblage. Characteristics of broad, squat proportions, the use of hard-hammer percussion and the scarce use of platform preparation, which is common to the majority of flake removals, would be most consistent with flintwork from the Late Neolithic and Bronze Age. Of the 90 flake removals, the majority are overwhelmingly tertiary (64 pieces or 71%) compared with 17 which are secondary, and nine primary flakes. This would suggest that primary reduction was undertaken elsewhere, and that most flaking related to tool manufacture or repair.

Discussion

The group associated with tree-throw pit 1005 comprises mainly non-retouched flakes, the fresh condition of which is consistent with this being contemporary with the associated Beaker pottery. The size and range of the lithics assemblage is indicative of earlier prehistoric activity more substantial than might be suggested from the single surviving Period 1 feature, and it appears that the location was a focus for activity beginning as early the Mesolithic. Given the domestic character of the Beaker pottery, it is tempting to ascribe the bulk of the redeposited lithics to this period. The evidence relating to this period is typically sparse, but could signify seasonal or semi-permanent habitation.

Catalogue of illustrated flint (Fig. 7)

No. 1   Mesolithic adze from unpatinated mid/darker grey flint. The cutting edge is damaged, but some suggestion of tranchet sharpening to the ventral. Length 158mm. Period 3, ditch 1338 (fill 1339).

No. 2   Microlith (broken). Obliquely blunted. White-patinated flint. Length 20mm. Period 3, ditch 1338 (fill 1339).

No. 3   Crested blade (broken). Dark grey flint with mottled patina. Length 38mm. Period 4, pit 2021 (fill 2020).

No. 4   Leaf-shaped arrowhead (broken). Ogival form? Unpatinated dark grey flint. Length 26mm. Period 3, pit 1676 (fill 1675).

Beaker Pottery, by E.R. McSloy

The Beaker pottery (57 sherds; 416g) relates to a single feature, Period 1 tree-throw pit 1005. A minimum of eight vessels are represented. The Rim EVEs value is 0.79.

Fabrics

Three types of pottery fabric are present. Full descriptions of the fabrics are available in the archive.

BKG   Medium/coarse grog. Common, moderately sorted and subangular grog 1–3mm.
BKGf   Fine grog. Sparse fine, well sorted grog (0.5–1mm) in silty matrix.
BKGq   Common, well sorted and subangular grog 1–2mm; sparse, moderately subangular quartzite 0.5–1.5mm.

Condition and description

The condition of the Beaker group is mixed with some surface loss. Fineware vessels (Fig. 8, nos. 1–3) are thinner walled and exhibit impressed-comb decoration; the coarsewares are thicker and undecorated or with fingernail 'rustication'.

The level of fragmentation makes classification and stylistic comparisons difficult. The concave neck exhibited by vessel no. 1, and the banded impressed-comb decoration seen with vessels nos. 1–3, are characteristics of Style 2 (middle Beaker phase) as defined by Case (1993), as is the occurrence of rusticated (fingernail-decorated) vessels (nos. 4–7). Although absolute dating programmes have cast some doubt on the validity of the early/middle/late divisions (Kinnes *et al.* 1991), a date in the final quarter of the 3rd millennium BC, or a little after, is probable.

Little, if any, Beaker pottery has been recorded previously from the Severn Vale (Darvill

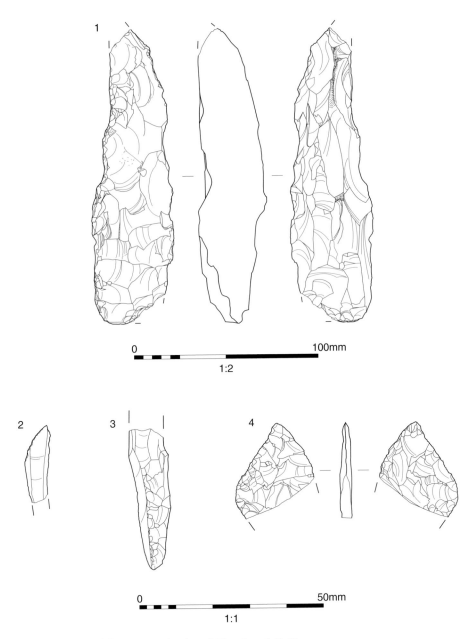

Fig. 7   Worked flint, No. 1 (1:2) and Nos. 2 to 4 (1:1)

1984; 2006) and the material described here represents a significant discovery. Although from a seemingly 'non-funerary' deposit, the nature of the activity at Foxes Field is difficult to characterise. The mix of finewares and coarsewares suggests a 'domestic' group, and together with the (redeposited) lithics hints at evidence for settlement. The ephemeral nature of Beaker 'settlement' is, however, well understood (Gibson 1982).

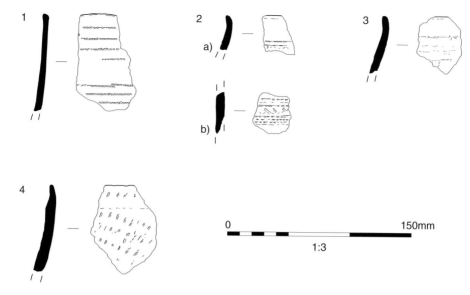

Fig. 8   Beaker pottery (1:3)

Catalogue (all from tree-throw pit 1005) (Fig. 8)

No. 1   Fabric BKGf. Rim (simple) and concave neck. Decoration consists of grouped bands of square-toothed comb impressions. (3 sherds; 30g; 0.08 EVEs).

No. 2   Fabric BKG. Out-curved rim and bodysherd. The bodysherd with impressed comb decoration as bands, and zone with crosshatch. (7 sherds; 24g; 0.05 EVEs).

No. 3   Fabric BKG. Weathered. Out-curved rim and bodysherds with indistinct banded decoration. (11 sherds; 28g; 0.05 EVEs).

No. 4   Fabric BKG. Concave neck; thickened/collar-like rim. Decoration as rows of impressed fingernail. (15 sherds; 184g; 0.05 EVEs).

No. 5   Fabric BKG. Bodysherds with indistinct banded decoration. (2 sherds; 28g). *Not illustrated.*

No. 6   Fabric BKG. Weathered. Thickened/collar-like rim, undecorated bodysherds and simple base. Thickness 9–9mm. (15 sherds; 85g; 0.06 EVEs). *Not illustrated.*

No. 7   Fabric BKGq. Thickened/collar-like rim; bodysherd with fingernail impressions in rows. (3 sherds; 26g; 0.10 EVEs). *Not illustrated.*

No. 8   Fabric BKGq. Bodysherd with indistinct comb impressions. (1 sherd; 11g). *Not illustrated.*

Roman Pottery, by E.R. McSloy

Pottery amounting to 5570 sherds (64.4kg) was recovered from 267 deposits. Further quantities (800 sherds) from the evaluation were not re-examined as part of this work; a report detailing that material can be found in the archive. The assemblage was quantified by sherd count, weight and a measure of surviving rim percentage: estimated vessel equivalents (EVEs). Coding for Roman types includes nomenclature for the National Roman Fabric Reference Collection (Tomber and Dore 1998). The assemblage was sorted into 30 fabrics (Table 2) defined according to primary inclusions and characteristics of firing. The majority conforms to established ware types, where source (or region) is known and for which the typological development in the repertoire is well understood.

Table 2: Roman pottery: summary quantifications by sherd count (Ct.) and weight (Wt.)
*codes as National Roman fabric reference collection (Tomber and Dore 1998)

Fabric	Description	Ct.	Wt.	Total EVEs	Period 2 Count	Ditch B Count	Ditch D Count	Midden H Count	Ditch A Count
GROG/LS	Grog with limestone	237	1062	-	237	-	-	-	-
GROGc	Coarse grog	157	1653	.52	4	7	69	2	11
MAL REB	Palaeozoic limestone	816	9586	4.40	388	84	105	34	16
MAL REA*	Malverns rock-tempered	1	3	-	-	-	-	-	-
SHELL	Fossil shell-tempered	1	4	-	1	-	-	-	-
GROGf	'Belgic' grog-tempered	135	1761	1.41	-	28	28	16	10
SVW OX2*	Severn Valley ware	1948	24208	16.60	-	124	97	88	514
SVW OXg	SVW (grog inclusions)	111	2758	.58	1	1	-	27	17
SVW OXo	SVW (charcoal inclusions)	189	3631	1.66	-	2	15	84	29
SVW RE	SVW (reduced)	16	207	-	-	13	-	-	1
DOR BB1*	Dorset Black-burnished	533	5015	6.38	-	3	-	-	168
LOC BS	North Wilts? black sandy	645	3458	4.61	-	71	102	14	185
SAV GT*	Savernake ware	97	2317	1.91	1	13	26	10	5
SOW WS*	South-west white slipped	11	160	.24	-	-	-	-	2
LEAD	Wilts lead glazed	1	6	.05	-	-	-	-	-
MISC CC	Misc. colour-coated	11	59	.19	-	-	-	-	-
OXID	Wilts oxidised	44	541	1.14	-	4	13	2	7
OX FF	Wilts oxidised (flagons)	24	307	.21	1	-	1	7	-
WH	Whitewares	5	28	.05	-	-	-	-	-
WS FF	White-slipped (flagons)	21	327	-	-	10	6	-	-
OXF RS*	Oxford red-slipped ware	3	6	.05	-	-	-	-	-
OXF WH*	Oxford whiteware	12	264	.42	-	1	-	-	2
BBIM	Late Black-burnished imitations	57	683	.59	-	-	-	-	-
GWc	Greywares (coarse sandy)	135	2055	1.21	-	3	4	-	16
GWf	Greywares (fine; sparse quartz)	155	1969	1.76	-	5	24	1	47
MIC GW	Micaceous greywares	125	1137	1.02	-	-	-	-	-
LGF SA	Samian (La Graufesenque)	9	59	.18	-	1	1	-	4
LEZ SA2	Samian (Lezoux)	46	303	.85	-	-	-	-	12
EG SA	Samian (east Gaulish)	13	91	.05	-	-	-	-	4
BAT AM2*	Baetican amphoras	12	815	-	-	-	-	-	-
Totals		*5570*	*64473*	*46.08*	*633*	*370*	*491*	*285*	*1050*

The larger part of the assemblage was derived from cut features, primarily ditches or gullies (2393 sherds; 43%) and pits (1649 sherds; 30%). Significant quantities also came from midden layers 1332 (midden J) and 1344 (midden H) (928 sherds; 17%). The rest of the assemblage was derived from cleaning layers, subsoil deposits, and from the fills of graves and furrows. The moderately high mean sherd weight (12g) for the Roman assemblage does not suggest high levels of disturbance. Surface survival tends to be poor, caused mostly by environmental factors rather than abrasion.

The pottery from both evaluation and excavation is broadly reflective of 'rural' site groups from the Severn Vale to the south of Gloucester. The dominance of jars (59.7% by EVEs) is a feature common to most Romano-British groups, though typically is more pronounced for rural sites. Lids occur sparsely (0.7%), although some further sherds with sooting may also be of this form. Open forms (20.4%) are mainly utilitarian classes in Black-burnished ware or Severn Valley ware, although there are a few platters (1.2%) from among the earliest groups. Drinking vessels are well represented (17.2%), this being typical of Severn Valley ware-dominated groups, where tankards and cups are usually prominent. By contrast, incidence of specialist forms comprising flagons (0.5%) and mortaria (1.4%) is low.

Fabric groups

Transitional and 'Belgic'-derived:
MAL REA; MAL REB; SHELL; GROGc; GROGf; GROG/LS

Transitional pottery (handmade types with Iron Age origin, persisting into the Roman period) makes up 22% of the total by count. Most or all are from the area of the Malvern Hills and comprise jars, with simple or everted-rim classes (Fig. 9, no. 1) and large hammer-rim forms (Fig. 9, no. 3). Wheelthrown, grog-tempered types, mostly necked bowls in the same tradition of 'Belgic' wares known in South East England as early as the 1st century BC, make up a further 2.5%.

Severn Valley ware: SVW OX2; SVW OXg; SVW OXo; SVW RE

This is the dominant coarseware tradition within the Severn Vale and wider region, current throughout the period. At Foxes Field it accounts for 43% of the total by count. Approximately half of identifiable vessels are jars; the majority (70%) are necked storage jar classes, the remainder are wide-mouthed forms (30%). The presence of early fabric variants (SVWOXg; SVWOXo), carinated cups/bowls (Webster 1976, Class H) and platters (ibid., Class K) support dating centring in the later 1st and 2nd centuries AD.

Micaceous greywares: MIC GW

Abundant in Gloucester and the Severn Vale. Dating to the later 3rd/4th century AD, its scarcity (just 2.2% overall) reflects reduced levels of activity at this site in this period.

Coarsewares: LOC BS; GWc; GWf; BBIM; OXID; SAV GT; SOW WS; DOR BB1; OXF WH

The modest quantities from the Savernake kilns (2% by count) include necked jars and neckless/bead-rim storage jars. Most abundant of the sandy reduced fabrics (12% of the total by count) are black-firing wares (fabric LOC BS), equivalent to 'local' Cirencester type 5 (Rigby 1982a). Sandy greywares and oxidised wares compare with North Wiltshire wares described from Cirencester (Rigby 1982b, fabrics 17/98). Probable Wiltshire type SOW WS is poorly represented, the sole identifiable form is a collared mortarium (cf. Rigby 1982b, fig. 43, no. 47) from hollow J. Dorset Black-burnished wares make up 10% of the assemblage total, within which jars predominate (66% by EVEs). Oxfordshire whitewares are uncommon, present as single examples of forms M3, M14 and M17 classes (Young 1977a).

Finewares and white-slipped/other flagon fabrics:
OX FF; WS FF; MISC CC; OXF RS; LEAD; WH

The small numbers of this type may be an underestimate, the result of poor surface survival. A vessel which retains a thin orange slip is campanulate cup (Fig. 9, no. 6), identified as a rare incidence of Caerleon ware

Table 3: Samian pottery quantifications as vessel count/rim EVEs

Generic form	Specific form	LGF SA	LEZ SA2	EG SA
cup	33	-	7/.35	-
	indet.	1/-	-	-
bowl (dec.)	37	1/-	1//.06	-
bowl	31r	-	2/-	-
	38	-	-	1/-
	indet.	-	-	1/-
dish	18	4/.18	-	-
	18/31	-	3/.01	-
	18/31r	-	1/.02	-
	31	-	5/.24	2/.05
	35	2/-	-	-
	35/36	-	1/-	-
	36	-	5/.17	-
	42	-	1/-	-
	indet.	-	2/-	-
indet.		1/-	18/-	9/-
Totals		**9/.18**	**46/.85**	**13/.05**

and of the first half of the 2nd century AD. Also unusual is a lead-glazed beaker (fabric LEAD; Fig. 9, no. 7). Colour-coated vessels, including bag-shaped beakers of Antonine type from Ditch A, may be North Wiltshire products. White-slipped flagon fabrics may also be North Wiltshire products or from the Gloucester area. Oxfordshire red-slipped wares, which are dateable after *c.* AD 270, are uncommon. Body sherds in a sandy whiteware (fabric WH) may also be from this source.

Samian: LGF SA; LEZ SA2; EG SA (Table 3)
The samian represents a small group: 68 sherds or 1.3% of the total. Included are nine sherds of South Gaulish (La Graufesenque: LGF SA) manufacture, suggesting some use before *c.* AD 110. Of the rest, 46 sherds are Central Gaulish (Lezoux: LEZ SA2), the remainder (13 sherds) of East Gaulish origin (EG SA). The majority probably pre-dates *c.* AD 160, an East Gaulish Drag. 38 from pit 1281 (fill 1280) being a probable exception. A find of note from the evaluation was a British samian dish Drag. 18/31 made at Pulborough, Sussex (identification made by J. Timby and J. Bird). This is a rare occurrence from Gloucestershire, although previously recorded from Sea Mills (Timby 1987).

Amphoras: BAT AM2
Amphora types are restricted to bodysherds in Baetican (southern Spanish) fabric BAT AM2.

Stratigraphy and dating

Period 2: Late Iron Age to Early Roman (1st century BC to 1st century AD)
The large bulk of the pottery belongs to the transitional handmade tradition. Jar no. 1 from pit 1100 is typical of the vessels in Malvern Hills limestone-tempered fabrics from the Late Iron Age and continuing as late as the AD 70s. Three large storage jars of the Late Iron Age/transitional wares set upright into pits 1369, 1388 and 1391 were possibly used for cold storage. Fully Romanised pottery found within pit 1388 included a collared flagon

of Claudian/Neronian type (Fig. 9, no. 2). This might suggest a post-Conquest date in this instance, although these sherds derive from the backfill.

Period 3: Roman (late 1st to 4th century AD)
Establishment of the enclosure by the end of the 1st century AD is indicated by large pottery groups associated with the initial use of Ditches B and D, together with deposit 1344 (midden H). Late Iron Age/transitional wares continue to be well-represented in this period, occurring alongside reduced coarsewares and Severn Valley ware. A few groups contain South Gaulish samian sherds of platter form 18, consistent with Flavian/Trajanic dating. A notable absence from such groups is Dorset Black-burnished ware (BB1), a strong indication for dating before *c*. AD 120.

The composition of pottery groups from the re-cuts of Ditch A is distinct from those of Ditches B and D. Together with groups from pit and gully features internal to the enclosure, this material indicates activity continuing well into the 2nd century AD. The scarcity of Late Iron Age/transitional types is very apparent from the 2nd-century AD groups, as is the abundance of Dorset Black-burnished ware and the routine presence of Central Gaulish samian. Dorset Black-burnished ware forms are mainly jars with acute-angled lattice (Seager-Smith and Davies 1993, types 1–2) with fewer dishes with plain or moulded rims (ibid., types 20 and 22). Severn Valley wares are abundant from these deposits, mainly as jars and tankards; the latter with straight or slightly flaring walls and lattice decoration typical of the 2nd century AD (Fig. 9, no. 8).

Evidence from the pottery for dating after *c*. AD 220/250 is scarce and material of this date is absent from the fills of the enclosure ditches. The large group from hollow J contains some late elements including late Dorset Black-burnished ware forms, although this group is well broken-up and disturbance is suspected. Quantities of micaceous greyware MIC GW are small overall (2.2% by count), and compare with 21% (by weight) at Frocester, a site with significant activity into the 4th century AD (Timby 2000). Rectangular pit 2120 alone contained a moderately large pottery group suggesting a date in the late 3rd or 4th century AD (64 sherds), including 27 sherds of micaceous greyware occurring as Dorset Black-burnished-derived dishes and jars. Also present were a late form Black-burnished ware jar and sherds of Oxford red-slipped ware, the sole occurrence from the assemblage.

Summary
Overall the assemblage is unexceptional in its composition and compares to that from the earlier Roman phases at Frocester (Timby 2000). The small size of the samian group (just 1.3% by count) and the utilitarian character of the coarse pottery are indications that the earlier Roman assemblage relates to a low-status community. The earliest (Period 2) activity may contain some pre-Roman material among the Late Iron Age/transitional wares, though a date of around the Conquest would seem more likely. Pottery relating to major landscape features Ditches B and D probably dates to the later 1st century AD. That from Ditch A is significantly later, probably dating to the middle or later 2nd century AD. The apparent disconnect implies that Ditch A is a later addition, or is the result of re-cutting. Activity within the enclosed area dates across the late 1st and 2nd centuries AD; the large midden deposits suggest domestic activity nearby. There is little evidence for substantive activity past *c*. AD 200 from the pottery assemblage, and it seems very likely that the enclosure was abandoned as a settlement well before its use for burial, probably in the 4th century AD.

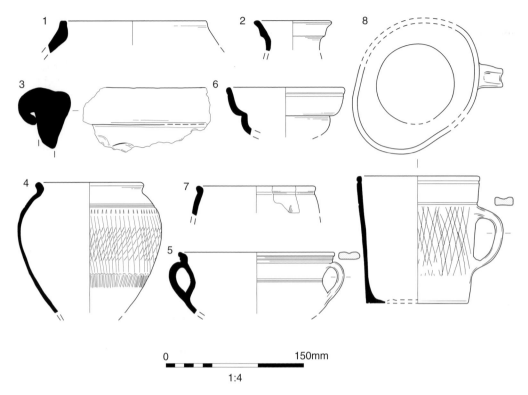

Fig. 9   Roman pottery (1:4)

Catalogue of illustrated sherds (Fig. 9)

Period 2

No. 1   Jar with upright/internally-bevelled rim. Fabric MAL REB. Pit 1100 (fill 1101).
No. 2   Collared flagon. Pit 1388 (fill 1389). Fabric OX FF.

Period 3

No. 3   Large storage jar; hammer-rim (cf. Spencer 1983, fig. 3). Fabric GROGc. Ditch D (fill 1639).
No. 4   Ovoid beaker (cf. Rigby 1982a, fig. 51, no. 52). Fabric LOG GWf. Ditch D (fill 1275).
No. 5   Handled bowl. Fabric OXID. Ditch D (fill 1137).
No. 6   Campanulate cup (Drag.27 copy). Fabric MISC CC (Caerleon ware?). Gully 1606 (fill 1607).
No. 7   Beaker or cup? attributable to Arthur's Wanborough group (Arthur 1978, 319–24, fig. 8.8, no. 8.2). Wiltshire glazed ware. Pit 1564 (fill 1482).
No. 8   Tankard (cf. Webster 1976; class E39). Probable second (distorted). Severn Valley ware. Ditch 1199 (fill 1200).

Metalwork and worked antler, by E.R. McSloy

A total of 575 items of metal and one of worked antler were recovered. Items of intrinsic interest are described, with full details of the remaining items in the archive. The vast majority (554 items) are of iron. The majority comprise nails or fragmentary items of uncertain use. 'Household' objects include three knives, one of which (from Period 3 pit

1622) is classifiable by its form (Manning's Type 23; 1985, 118). Agricultural implements include a fragmentary ploughshare from Period 3 gully 1606 and a shears blade from pit 2120. The latter is of Manning's Type 2 (1985, 34) and of a size suitable for sheep shearing or crafts use. Hollow J, which produced smithing-related ironworking waste, also produced large quantities of ironwork (48 items). A number of structural fittings were recorded from this deposit including two 'holdfasts' and a T-clamp, together with 33 nails.

Objects of copper alloy (16 in total) comprise personal dress/toilet items as well as fragmentary/unidentifiable material. From Period 3 Ditch D is a Colchester-derivative brooch of Polden Hill type (not illustrated). It belongs to Mackreth's transitional type 2(a) (2011, 70–1) and probably dates to the later 1st or early 2nd century AD.

The single worked antler object, recovered from Period 3 pit 2120, consists of a red deer antler tine, 125mm in length and perforated for suspension. It has been worn smooth from use or handling and may represent a weaving implement or piercing tool.

Grave finds

A total of 54 nails derived from graves, with larger groups from graves 1530 (13 nails) 2110 (6) and 2113 (32), indicating the use of wooden coffins. Clusters of iron hobnails were associated with graves 1158, 1167, 1171, 1193, 1217 and 2113, and represent the remains of nailed footwear worn, rather than placed, within the grave. In addition, iron shoe 'cleats', some of unusual form, were recorded from grave 1144 (Fig. 10, no. 2).

Other than the nailed footwear, a coin from grave 1193 and iron cleaver from grave 1171 (No. 1, below) were the only objects deposited as 'grave goods'. Knives and cleavers are uncommon Romano-British grave finds (Philpott 1991, 176–7). Most known examples date to the Late Roman period.

Catalogue of illustrated metalwork (Fig. 10)
Iron

No. 1   Iron cleaver. Socketed. The blade back is level with the socket and continues this line to the tip. The blade edge is strongly convex. No. 1 compares to Roman type 1B cleavers described by Manning (1985, 122). The rounded notch at the junction of the socket and blade is however untypical. A similar socketed cleaver from Cirencester is also a grave find (*Antiquaries Journal* 1927, 321). Length 255mm; width (max): 72mm; diameter at socket 30mm. Period 3, grave 1171.

No. 2   Iron shoe cleats (x10). Two or possibly three cleats are of the same form as the illustrated example, which features a conical projection. The remainder are plain and compare with examples from Kingscote (Scott 1998, 165). Width 16–18mm. Period 3, grave 1144.

Copper alloy

No. 3   Umbonate plate brooch with hinged pin in place. Variant of Macketh's British Plate series including gilded types 3.b.6 (2011, 162–3) and round, single-zoned brooches. No. 3 is a simple example of the class, without tooled decoration, and all traces of original gilding seemingly lost. Dating for the class concentrates in the mid-2nd to mid-3rd century AD. Diameter 22–24mm. Period 4, furrow 1228.

No. 4   Nail cleaner. Blade is straight for most of its length, with a slight expansion towards its tip. The perforated head is semicircular, with rectangular mouldings below, decorated with single and double transverse grooves. All faces of the blade have fine grooves bordering the longer sides. No. 4 matches Eckardt and Crummy's loosely agglomerated 'straight-sided nail cleaners with varying decoration' (2008, 134–5), and resembles an example illustrated from Woodeaton, Oxon. (Kirk 1949, fig. 6.6). Probably 2nd century AD. Length 52mm; width 5mm. Period 3, pit 1513.

No. 5   Penannular bracelet with 'snake's head' terminals (Johns' Type Bii, Johns 1996). The surviving head is diamond-shaped, separated from the hoop by a raised collar. The spine of the hoop and

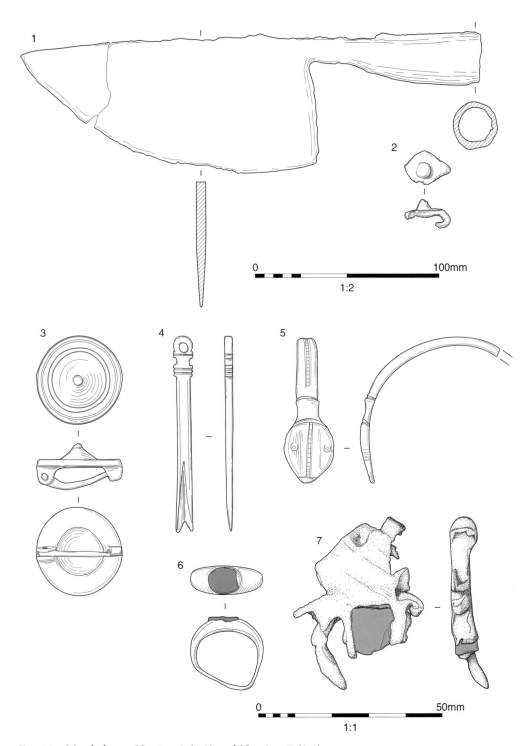

Fig. 10   Metal objects, Nos 1 to 2 (1:2) and Nos. 3 to 7 (1:1)

the centreline of the head feature groove-defined 'rope' decoration. The snake's mouth is shown as a groove and the eyes as punched circles. 'Serpentine' bracelets belong to the 1st to 3rd century AD (Johns 1996, 44). No. 5 is near identical to a bracelet from Hertfordshire (Watters 2011, BH-343C86). Width (head) 14mm; width (hoop) 5mm. Period 3, gully 1606.

No. 6   Finger ring. Oval hoop expanding towards the bezel. Plain oval setting of opaque blue glass. Henig's (1978) dating for this class (type 2) is the later 1st to 2nd centuries AD. Pottery supports dating in second half of the 2nd century AD. Width across hoop 20mm; width at bezel 7 mm. Period 3, Ditch A.

Lead alloy

No. 7   Fragment from flat object with square settings. One setting retains a samian *tessera*. The use of samian in mosaic pavements is well known, and 'curated' material may have been used following cessation of imports by the mid-3rd century AD. The use of lead as a bedding medium is unusual. Use for repair or as part of a removable panel (Jörn Schuster, pers. comm.) are possibilities. Length 45mm. Period 3, hollow J (layer 1332).

Coins, by E.R. McSloy

Iron Age (silver)

No. 1   Silver unit. Uninscribed 'Dobunnic D'; van Arsdell 1049–1 (*c*. 30–15 BC) (van Arsdell 1989); Mack 379 (Mack 1975). A redeposited find, occurring from the same deposit as radiate no. 2 and quantities of later Roman pottery. Period 3, pit 2120.

Roman (copper alloy)

No. 2   Gallienus radiate, AD 260–68. As RIC V 584, details uncertain. Period 3, pit 2120.

No. 3   Helena AE3, AD 324–30. Securitas Reipublicae; Trier (STR). LRBR 35. Recovered from the head area of inhumation 1195, and seems likely to have been placed in the mouth; the most common location for coins from graves up to the AD 350s (Philpott 1991, 212). The coin is unworn and retains its silvery wash, an indication that it may have been new when deposited. Period 3, grave 1193.

No. 4   AE4 copy. Fallen horseman type, AD 353–54 (or later). Period 3, Hollow J (layer 1332).

Worked stone, by Fiona Roe

Introduction

The worked stone was examined with a x10 hand lens to determine the lithic materials, which are varied, though none are unusual occurrences in Gloucestershire. Nine Roman worked-stone objects were identified, together with 16 or more small fragments of building stone. There are also 150 fragments of burnt stone, mostly small in size. In addition to these finds, a prehistoric pebble-hammer was recovered during the evaluation (Young 2009a, 17).

Stone objects

There are pieces from five rotary querns, all made of Upper Old Red Sandstone from the Wye Valley/Forest of Dean area. This Old Red Sandstone is variable in character, so that these querns were made variously from plain sandstone (No. 3), pebbly sandstone (Nos. 2 and 5) and quartz conglomerate (Nos. 1 and 4). The quartz conglomerate quern (No. 1), a near-complete lower stone, is a rare find, as it has a residual piece of the iron spindle fixed into the hole with lead, with some additional plaster (Fig. 11, also cover image). With a diameter of around 440mm, this lower stone would have been above average in size, but the other four querns were on the small side, with estimated diameters of between 360mm and 390mm. The complete lower stone (No. 1) and half of a smaller lower stone (No. 5) may have been deliberately placed in pit 2120.

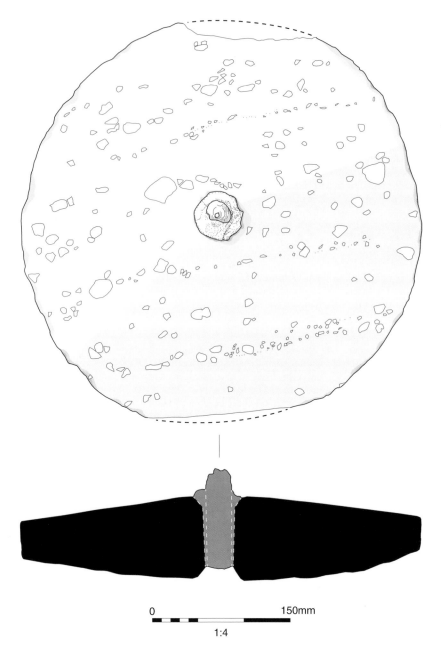

Fig. 11   Quern stone from pit 2120 (1:4)

The single whetstone (No. 7) consists of a variety of fine-grained calcareous sandstone that has often been attributed to the Cretaceous Kentish Rag. Recent detailed study has now shown that such whetstones were made from a different Cretaceous sandstone that occurs in the Weald Clay formation (Allen and Scott, forthcoming). It is a well-worn fragment of the rod variety and can be matched by similar whetstones currently known from at least 14 other Roman sites in Gloucestershire, as well as from many other Roman sites generally.

A fragment of imported Kimmeridge shale was recovered from hollow J. This shale, often in the form of bracelets, is frequently recorded from Gloucestershire Roman sites, as indeed elsewhere, however the find from Foxes Field is part of a fairly thick, flat object and so may come from the base of a dish or otherwise may have belonged to a tray or table top.

Two Roman objects are made from stone with a local provenance. A polisher recovered from the overlying subsoil consists of part of a quartzite pebble with particularly marked polish on the two main surfaces. Such polishers are common on Roman sites, with examples known from at least 17 sites in Gloucestershire alone, and a 2nd-century AD date for this item is probable. The glossy surfaces may have been caused by wear from smoothing textiles such as linen. A naturally perforated piece of shelly limestone from Ditch D may have been utilised as a loomweight. The broken half of a pebble-hammer with an hourglass hole from the evaluation was originally identified (incorrectly) as a stone macehead (Young 2009a, 17). Approximately half of the object is present, made from red crystalline sandstone, and is broken across the central hourglass perforation. Pebble-hammers of this type span the Mesolithic to Bronze Age periods and are often found redeposited. They are common generally and often made from quartzite pebbles (Roe 1979, 36, figs 14, 15).

Building stone

No stone-built domestic structures were identified at the site, but a few small pieces of building stone suggest that Roman buildings existed within the vicinity. The majority of the building stone is of local provenance. Both Lias and calcareous sandstone could have been used for construction, and the same two materials may have been further utilised for paving. Not all structures need have been thatched, since ceramic roofing tile was recorded. Two pieces of roofing tile consist of Pennant sandstone, which could have come from the Forest of Dean area if not from the Bristol Coalfield. While this sandstone may have been utilised for a complete roof, it may alternatively have been made into a decorative feature, as dark red bands in contrast with lighter-coloured roofing tiles of local limestone or calcareous sandstone.

Burnt stone

There is some 7kg of burnt stone, nearly half of which came from midden I, while the remainder was dispersed in pits and ditches throughout the site. Burnt stone is common generally on prehistoric sites and it seems likely that most of it relates to previous Iron Age or Late Iron Age/Early Roman activity on the site.

Discussion

The worked stone conforms to finds that have been recorded from other Gloucestershire Roman sites, suggesting an altogether conservative element of lithic usage in this area. The imported stone found at Foxes Field, consisting of Upper Old Red Sandstone, Pennant sandstone, Wealden sandstone and Kimmeridge shale, can all be matched at nearby Frocester Court (Price 2000; 2010) and at numerous other Gloucestershire Roman sites (Roe 2007). Roman rotary querns made from Old Red Sandstone are particularly common, being widely distributed both within and outside the Cotswold area (Shaffrey 2006). The burnt stone may represent the continued Iron Age and earlier prehistoric practice of cooking with heated stones, and the building stone is characteristic of an area where

Jurassic limestone was widely used for construction and roofing. The occurrence at Foxes Field of both Old Red Sandstone and Pennant sandstone may be linked with the evidence for ironworking at the site, since iron ore may also have been obtained from the Forest of Dean. In conclusion, the worked stone from this site is typical of local Roman sites, while further comparisons can be made over a wider area.

Worked Stone catalogue

No. 1   Rotary quern lower stone (Fig. 11). Upper Old Red Sandstone, quartz conglomerate. Nearly complete. Large disc style rotary quern with residual fragment of iron spindle fixed into central hole, damage to rim in two places, rim otherwise pecked to shape, convex grinding surface prepared by pecking and with traces of wear around edges, underside roughly trimmed to shape ; thickness at rim 52mm, diameter 440mm. Weight 23.6kg. Period 3, pit 2120.

No. 2   Rotary quern lower stone. Upper Old Red Sandstone, pebbly sandstone. Part of thick Iron Age-style rotary quern. Rim and underside damaged, convex grinding surface well prepared by pecking and only slightly worn, fully bored hour-glass spindle hole; max thickness 88mm, diameter < 380mm. Weight 6000g. Period 3, pit 1394.

No. 3   Rotary quern upper stone. Upper Old Red Sandstone, sandstone. Segment from Roman disc-style quern. Slightly concave grinding surface prepared by pecking in radial lines and with wear around rim area. Top surface shaped by chisel marks, small hollow around central hole for rynd, rim shaped by pecking; maximum thickness 51mm, diameter *c*. 370mm. Weight 2117g. Period 3, pit 1474.

No. 4   Rotary quern upper stone. Upper Old Red Sandstone, quartz conglomerate. Segment from Roman disc-style quern. Slightly concave grinding surface with traces of pecking, also traces of pecking into shape on top surface and rim; maximum thickness 61mm, diameter *c*. 390mm. Weight 2201g. Period 3, pit 1608.

No. 5   Rotary quern lower stone. Upper Old Red Sandstone, pebbly sandstone. Almost half of a Roman disc-style quern stone. Convex grinding surface with traces of wear into rings. Neatly pecked into shape, round rim, fully bored by a narrow hole, underside uneven with traces of burning; maximum thickness 69mm, diameter *c*. 360mm. Weight 4748g. Period 3, pit 2120.

No. 6   Fragment of quartzite pebble with two sides worked to a very high gloss from use as a polisher; 66mm x 37mm x 35mm. Weight 125g. Period 4 (subsoil).

No. 7   Whetstone. Wealden sandstone. Segment of whetstone, unevenly worn, originally rod variety; 64mm x 29mm x 25mm. Weight 64g. Period 3, pit 1705.

No. 8   Object fragment. Kimmeridge shale. Slightly burnt, no working traces remain. 67mm x 38mm x 18mm. Weight 49g. Period 3, hollow J.

Metallurgical Residues, by Sarah Paynter

Introduction

A total of 11.9kg of metalworking waste was recovered from the excavation, adding to the 5.7kg of material from the evaluation trenches (Young 2009a), and provides evidence for smithing utilising coal as fuel, and for smelting. Whilst most of the slag was found in Period 3 (Roman) contexts, the morphology of some of the smelting slag is atypical for the Roman period. A very small quantity was found in a Period 2 (Late Iron Age/ Early Roman) context; the remainder, from Period 4 (medieval to modern) contexts, was probably disturbed from Roman features by later agricultural practices.

Approximately 74% of the ironworking assemblage (by weight) from the excavation came from Period 3 hollow J. Features in the same area such as pit 1534 (fill 1532) and gully 1606 (fill 1605) accounted for a further 8% (by weight) of the assemblage. The assemblage was examined, divided into technological categories and weighed by context (Table 4). Waste from both iron-smelting and iron-smithing processes was identified.

Table 4: Summary metallurgical residues by category and Period (quantities as weight in grammes)

Process	Category	Period 2	Period 3	Period 4	Unphased	Total
Smelting	Flowed slag	-	451	567	81	1099
	Dense slag	-	1456	-	-	1456
Smithing	Hearth bottom (SHB)	-	2068	-	-	2068
Indeterminate	Undiagnostic slag	27	6571	63	-	6661
Other material	Vitrified lining	26	230	-	-	256
	Iron-rich stone	-	24	-	-	24
	Coal	-	9	-	-	9
Total	*Total*	*53*	*10809*	*630*	*81*	*11573*

Results: smelting

Roughly a quarter of the assemblage, comprising flowed slags and material described as 'dense' slag, can be attributed with greater or lesser certainty to iron smelting. Evidence for unused ore is sparse; restricted to fragments (24g) of iron-rich stone from pit 1725.

Flowed slags are characteristic of tapping furnaces, where the molten slag was 'tapped' through a hole at the base of the furnace. The slags produced are distinctive, exhibiting flow marks on the upper surface. Furnaces of this type are known from the Late Iron Age throughout the Roman period, and again from around the mid-medieval period onwards. Approximately half (567g) of the flowed slag was derived from Period 4 furrows or from the subsoil. The largest context group is that from hollow J (345g), with small quantities identified from grave 1158 (22g) and Ditch F (79g).

A slightly larger proportion of the smelting slags (1456g; compared to 1099g of flowed slag) consists of 'dense slag'. This material is considered to be characteristic of the use of non-tapping furnaces, or slag-pit furnaces, where the slag collected during the smelt in the bottom of the furnace or in a pit below the furnace shaft. Slag from non-tapping furnaces solidifies in large cakes, which sometimes contain impressions of straw or large pieces of wood. These cakes can break into lumps of dense iron slag. In England, non-tapping furnaces were used in the Iron Age and early medieval periods (Paynter 2006; 2007).

The distribution of the dense slag shows little correspondence with that of the flowed slag; only hollow J, productive of 74% of the metallurgical residues overall, included quantities from each class. The largest quantities relate to pit 1534 (837g) and a gully to the north of Ditch F (400g), with the residue from ditch 1338 and pit 1709.

Smithing

Evidence for iron smithing (the working or reworking of iron implements) is present most obviously in the form of smithing hearth bottom slags (SHBs). This category of material, formed in the base of smithing hearths during use, tends to a characteristic morphology, with a fairly flat top, a bowl-shaped bottom and a spongy texture. SHB slags weighing 2068g were identified only from hollow J.

Evidence for iron smithing in the form of microscopic residues (hammerscale) was sought from the numerous processed soil sample residues. Many contained small quantities of magnetic material but this was mostly fired clay or stone; however, the backfill (1159) of grave 1158 also contained several grammes of hammerscale. This grave was located just to the north of the large deposit of ironworking waste in hollow J.

Pieces of coal (9g in total) were also found on the site, in a variety of features (hollow J; Ditch F; gully 1572 and pit 1810), and may relate to its use for smithing. Coal fuel has occasionally been noted on other Roman sites near to coal sources (Dearne and Branigan 1995). Coal is not suitable for smelting.

General ironworking waste

The large bulk of the metallurgical waste (6661g; 56% by weight) lacked diagnostic characteristics and could not be assigned to a particular process. By far the largest group (5676g) came from hollow J with the remainder occurring in small quantities (up to 205g) from numerous other Period 3 features. In addition to this material, quantities of slag-coated fired clay, (or 'vitrified lining') were recovered, which could have come from furnace or hearth structures. A small quantity (26g) of this material was found in small pit 1224, from which Late Iron Age to Early Roman pottery was also recovered.

Discussion

The recovered ironworking slags include material relating to both smelting and smithing, with additional (larger) quantities that are indeterminate of process. Slag classes exclusively indicative for smithing were recovered only from hollow J or from features (grave 1158) located close to hollow J. The evidence for iron smelting was more generally distributed, with some material redeposited in Period 4 deposits. The pattern of activity, indicative of limited-scale iron production and smithing, is reflected locally at Frocester, where it dates from the later Iron Age and throughout the Roman period (Standing 2000, 92–4). The apparent use of coal as a fuel for smithing was not noted at Frocester, although its use in the Forest of Dean and south-east Wales is well attested (Young 2009b, 155–9).

Though the volume of ironworking residues from Period 3 deposits indicates that iron-working activities took place nearby, no metalworking features could be identified. A number of features near the southern edge of Ditch A had either *in situ* scorching or heated material deposited within them, but there was no evidence in the form of charcoal, slag-rich deposits or reduction-firing to link them with metalworking. The mass of ironworking waste relating to hollow J probably represents a secondary dump, possibly intended as metalling or hard standing.

Although it is very difficult to date slag by its morphology, selected characteristics of the (dense) smelting slags are inconsistent with the Roman dating suggested by the site phasing. Moreover the smelting slag from the evaluation, although some of it had flowed, is not typical tapping slag: it is more likely to have been produced by a non-tapping furnace of the type common in the Iron Age or Early Medieval periods. Given that there was some Late Iron Age activity at the site, but no evidence for early medieval activity, and that the features where the slag was found are generally Roman, a Late Iron Age or Early Roman date for the smelting is considered likely.

THE BIOLOGICAL EVIDENCE

Human bone, by Jonny Geber

A total of 15 Roman skeletons (Period 3) was discovered (see *Grave Catalogue*, below). The remains display a varying state of preservation and many skeletons are anatomically incomplete. The remains were analysed following standard recommended practices and osteological methodologies (Brickley and McKinley 2004; Buikstra and Ubelaker 1994; Ferembach *et al.* 1980). Living stature was estimated from long bone lengths using the equations by Trotter and Gleser (1952; 1958). For pathological frequencies, only true prevalence rates were calculated. Dentitions were quantified as observable when at least 25% were preserved and available for assessment; the vertebral column when >50% of the cervical, thoracic or lumbar spine was present. Details of the analyses are available in the archive.

Population characteristics

Of the 15 skeletons identified, two were non-adults and the remainder adults, of which seven could be sexed as females and five as males. The youngest individual in this group was an incomplete neonate skeleton (Sk 2135) comprising some skull vault fragments, ribs and right scapula and humerus, buried in a pit (1600), and possibly represents charnel from a burial disturbed in antiquity. The second non-adult skeleton belonged to an older child (Sk 1166), aged approximately 10 years at the time of death. Of the adults in this group, males appear to have lived longer than females, with the majority belonging to the older adult age category (≥46 years). Females, on the other hand, were primarily between 35 and 45 years of age at the time of death.

The living stature could be estimated in eleven adult skeletons. The females ranged in height from 154cm (5ft 1in) to 162cm (5ft 4in) with a mean height of 158cm (5ft 2in). Males measured between 163cm (5ft 4in) and 189cm (6ft 2in) in height, with a mean stature of 174cm (5ft 9in). These statures corroborate well with the estimated mean heights observed in Romano-British skeletal populations elsewhere across Britain (Roberts and Cox 2003).

Dental disease

Amongst these skeletons, only adult dentitions displayed evidence of dental disease. Tooth decay, or caries, was identified in all available dentitions, which were present in eleven individuals. In total, 27% (43/160) of all available teeth and 49% (24/49) of all molar teeth were affected. Mineralised plaque, known as calculus or tartar, was mostly observed on the anterior teeth in all adult dentitions. It tends to accumulate more in individuals with a diet rich in protein and carbohydrates (Roberts and Manchester 2005).

Nine individuals (9/11) displayed evidence of periodontal disease; in five this was moderate and in four it was severe. Age and sex did not appear to influence the severity in this group. Further pathologies of the jaws were represented by two identified cases of periapical lesions, which comprised a granuloma in the dentition of an older adult male (Sk 1179) and a chronic abscess in an older adult female (Sk 1191). Both conditions originate from an infection that gains entry to the dental pulp via caries, attrition or trauma (Dias *et al.* 2007; Dias and Tayles 1997). While granulomae are generally asymptomatic (Hillson 2005), abscesses may result in serious and painful ailments (Ayoub 2010; Hillson 2005).

Dental caries, and to some degree periodontal disease, are the likely causes of antemortem tooth loss in this population. Teeth had been lost before death in ten adults, which represented 24% (60/250) of all alveoli (teeth sockets) and 44% (39/88) of all molar teeth alveoli. The most severe case was observed in the incomplete dentition of an adult of unknown sex (Sk 1146), where nine of 21 observable alveoli revealed evidence of teeth having been lost in life.

Joint disease

Diseases of the joints are normally the result of continuing wear-and-tear of the articulations, and tend to increase in both distribution and severity with age. It was present, in some form, in eight adult skeletons, primarily affecting the hips, shoulders and hands. Osteoarthritis presented as eburnated (polished) articulations (Rogers *et al.* 1987) in the wrists of two older adult males (Sk 1190, Sk 1195) and the hands of an older adult female (Sk 1191). Osteoarthritis was also diagnosed in the cervical and upper thoracic vertebrae in Sk 1191, Sk 1195 and Sk 1529, also of skeletally advanced age.

The spine was affected by joint disease in ten adults (10/11). Seven individuals displayed evidence of vertebral osteophytosis or 'spondylosis deformans', which occurs from compression of the spine due to lost elasticity of the vertebral plates (Rogers *et al.* 1985). Two of these individuals (Sk 1179, Sk 1195) were also affected by a related degenerative condition in the neck vertebrae (osteochondrosis) (Kelley 1982).

Ossification of the ligamentum flavum, which have the primary function of maintaining an upright posture to the spine, was observed in the thoracic spines of seven individuals. Although rarely reported upon, this is a common spinal pathology in archaeological skeletons reflecting instability of the vertebral column (Kudo *et al.* 1983).

Three females and three males were affected by so-called Schmorl's nodes in the lower thoracic and the lumbar vertebrae. It is often a completely asymptomatic condition (Faccia and Williams 2008), and there has been debate on whether this pathology should be considered as a degenerative condition, related to trauma, or simply as a congenital spinal anomaly (Dar *et al.* 2010; Saluja *et al.* 1986).

Metabolic disease

An older adult male (Sk 1173) was the only skeleton with clear evidence of metabolic disease, manifested as porotic lesions on the roof of the eye orbits (cribra orbitalia), which is believed to relate to Vitamin B12 and C deficiency, as well as iron deficiency anaemia (Oxenham and Cavill 2010; Stuart-Macadam 1991; Walker *et al.* 2009). The same skeleton also displayed healed periostitis on the tibiae, which may also relate to a metabolic disease process. Periostitis is a common pathology found in association with Vitamin C deficiency or scurvy (Brickley and Ives 2008; Geber and Murphy 2012; van der Merwe *et al.* 2010), but could also be the result of infection.

Infectious disease

One older adult female (Sk 1157) displayed a possible case of bilateral mastoiditis, resulting from an acute middle ear infection (otitis media) (Flohr and Schultz 2009a; 2009b); potentially an extremely painful condition with other symptoms such as fever and head ache.

Two adults, a female (Sk 1173) and a male (Sk 1179) displayed a build-up of reactive bone on the floor of the sinuses, indicating chronic sinusitis. This is commonly attributed to poor air quality and pollution (Boocock *et al.* 1995; Lewis *et al.* 1995; Roberts 2007). Further evidence of respiratory disease suggesting a pulmonary infection was found in two individuals (Sk 1164, Sk 1166). These included child skeleton 1166, which displayed active proliferation of new bone on the visceral surface of the neck and body of a minimum of four left ribs. One male (Sk 1164) was affected on a minimum of two left and two right ribs. Diseases such as pneumonia, tuberculosis, actinomycosis and hypertrophic osteoarthropathy are known to result in rib lesions of this kind (Kelley and Micozzi 1984; Lambert 2002; Matos and Santons 2006; Mays *et al.* 2002).

Trauma

Five skeletons displayed evidence of trauma. The most apparent injury was a healed so-called 'Colles' fracture of the distal radius in the right wrist of an adult female (Sk 2111). This type of injury is a frequent consequence of a fall onto an outstretched hand, and is a common fracture treated in hospitals today (Nijs and Broos 2004). Two skeletons displayed healed intra-articular fractures, which were identified in the axis vertebra and talus (of the spine) in an adult female (Sk 1173), and a proximal phalanx of the left hand of an adult male (Sk 1195).

Two individuals, a male (Sk 1179) and a female (Sk 1216), were affected by osteochondritis dissecans on the distal humeri joints in the right elbows. This condition is most commonly initiated by trauma (Aufderheide and Rodríguez-Martín 1998; Ortner 2003). It is manifested as a defined pit lesion on a convex synovial joint surface.

Conclusion

The burials were mainly of adult individuals, which may suggest that non-adults and juveniles were generally interred elsewhere. Both males and females were present, and there does not appear to be any association between burial morphology and social categories such as age and gender. These skeletons displayed pathologies commonly observed in Romano-British skeletal populations, which included dental, joint and pulmonary disease, as well as trauma. The frequency of the dental pathologies appears to be relatively high (c.f. Roberts and Cox 2003), although this is likely to be a reflection of the demography of this population, as it comprised predominately aged adult individuals.

Grave Catalogue

Grave 1008 (Sk 1009) (Fig. 12)
Grave: W-E rectangular cut with squared corners and concave base. 1.05m x 0.45m, 0.1m deep.
Burial: flexed, 60% complete, moderate preservation.
Human Bone: young adult female, 17-25 years, 154cm.
Pathology summary: spinal DJD.
Dating: 2nd to 4th-century AD pottery.

Grave 1144 (Sk 1146) (Fig. 13)
Grave: NW-SE irregular cut, highly truncated, 1.1m x 0.9m, 0.2m deep.
Burial: crouched, 15% complete, poor preservation.
Human Bone: young adult, 36-45 years.
Pathology summary: caries, calculus, antemortem tooth loss, periodontal disease.
Grave Goods: cleats.
Dating: 3rd to 4th-century AD pottery; cleats typically 4th century AD.

*Fig. 12   Sk 1009 (grave 1008), looking north.
Scale 0.5m*

*Fig. 13   Sk 1146 (grave 1144), looking south-west.
Scale 1m*

Grave 1158 (Sk 1157) (Fig. 14)
Grave: S-N sub-oval cut with rounded corners and flat base. 1.8m x 0.75m, 0.28m deep.
Burial: supine, 50% complete, poor preservation.
Human Bone: adult female, 46+ years, 160cm.
Pathology summary: caries, calculus, antemortem tooth loss, periodontal disease, ?mastoiditis.
Grave Goods: hobnails, flint blade.
Dating: 3rd to 4th century AD pottery; Romano-British hobnails.

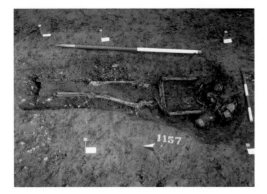

Fig. 14   Sk 1158 (grave 1157), looking east. Scales 1m and 0.4m

Grave 1165 (Sk 1164) (Fig. 15)
Grave: N-S rectangular cut with rounded corners and flattish base. 1.35m x 0.6m, 0.19m deep.
Burial: crouched, 90% complete, moderate preservation.
Human Bone: adult male, 36-45 years.
Pathology summary: caries, calculus, antemortem tooth loss, periodontal disease, DJD, spinal DJD, pulmonary infection.
Dating: late 1st to 2nd-century AD pottery.

Fig. 15   Sk 1164 (grave 1165), looking west. Scale 1m

Grave 1167 (Sk 1166) (Fig. 16)
Grave: N-S sub-rectangular cut with rounded corners and flat base. 1.0m x 0.45m, 0.04m deep.
Burial: supine, 70% complete, poor preservation.
Human Bone: child, 6-12 years.
Pathology summary: pulmonary infection.
Grave Goods: hobnails.
Dating: Romano-British pottery and hobnails.

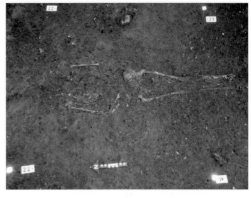

Fig. 16   Sk 1166 (grave 1167), looking east.

Grave 1171 (Sk 1173) (Fig. 17)
Grave: S-N rectangular cut with rounded corners and flat base. 1.7m x 0.54m, 0.2m deep.
Burial: flexed, 95% complete, very good preservation.
Human Bone: adult female, 36-45 years, 161cm.
Pathology summary: caries, calculus, antemortem tooth loss, periodontal disease, cribra orbitalia, sinusitis, spinal DJD, periostitis, trauma.
Grave Goods: hobnails, iron cleaver.
Dating: 2nd century or later pottery; 3rd to 4th-century AD cleaver; Romano-British hobnails.

Fig. 17   Sk 1173 (grave 1171), looking east. Scales 1m and 0.4m

Grave 1180 (Sk 1179) (Fig. 18)

Grave: SE-NW sub-oval cut with rounded corners and flat base. 1.55m x 0.54m, 0.34m deep.
Burial: supine, 85% complete, very good preservation.
Human Bone: adult male, 46+ years, 173cm.
Pathology summary: caries, calculus, granuloma, antemortem tooth loss, periodontal disease, sinusitis, DJD, spinal DJD, trauma.
Grave Goods: lead pot repair.
Dating: 3rd to 4th-century AD pottery.

Fig. 18   Sk 1179 (grave 1180), looking south-west. Scales 1m and 0.4m

Grave 1192 (Sk 1190) (see Fig. 6)

Grave: N-S sub-oval cut with rounded corners and a flat base. 1.6m x 1.0m, 0.13m deep. Contains two burials.
Burial: flexed, 85% complete, good preservation.
Human Bone: adult male, 46+ years, 171cm.
Pathology summary: caries, calculus, antemortem tooth loss, periodontal disease, DJD (osteoarthritis), spinal DJD.
Dating: later than Period 2 posthole 1211. Contemporary with Sk 1191.

Grave 1192 (Sk 1191) (see Fig. 6)

Grave: N-S sub-oval cut with rounded corners and a flat base. 1.6m x 1.0m, 0.13m deep. Contains two burials.
Burial: flexed, 80% complete, poor preservation.
Human Bone: adult female, 46+ years, 162cm.
Pathology summary: caries, calculus, abscess, antemortem tooth loss, periodontal disease, DJD (osteoarthritis), spinal DJD.
Dating: 1st-century AD pottery. Contemporary with Sk 1190.

Grave 1193 (Sk 1195) (Fig. 19)

Grave: SE-NW elongated oval cut with rounded corners and a rounded base. 1.9m x 0.45m, 0.12m deep.
Burial: prone, 75% complete, moderate preservation.
Human Bone: adult male, 46+ years, 189cm.
Pathology summary: caries, calculus, antemortem tooth loss, periodontal disease, DJD (osteoarthritis), spinal DJD (osteoarthritis), trauma.
Grave Goods: coin; hobnails.
Dating: coin AD 324-330; Romano-British pottery and hobnails.

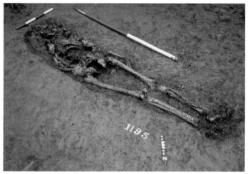

Fig. 19   Sk 1195 (grave 1193), looking south. Scales 1m and 0.4m

Grave 1217 (Sk 1216) (Fig. 20)

Grave: SE-NW rectangular cut with rounded corners and a flat base. 2.0m x 0.7m, 0.21m deep.
Burial: supine, 90% complete, moderate preservation.
Human Bone: adult female, 26-35 years, 160cm.
Pathology summary: caries, calculus, spinal DJD, trauma.
Grave Goods: hobnails; lead vessel/sheet.
Dating: 2nd to 3rd-century AD pottery; Romano-British hobnails.

Fig. 20   Sk 1216 (grave 1217), looking south-west. Scales 1m and 0.4m

Grave 1530 (Sk 1529) (Fig. 21)

Grave: SE-NW sub-rectangular cut with rounded corners and a flat base. 1.9m x 1.02m, 0.14m deep.
Burial: supine, 80% complete, poor preservation, coffin nails.
Human Bone: adult ?male, 26-35 years, 163cm.
Pathology summary: caries, DJD, spinal DJD (osteoarthritis).
Dating: Romano-British pottery.

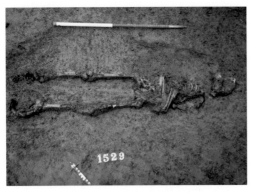

Fig. 21   Sk 1529 (grave 1530), looking north-east. Scale 1m

Grave 2110 (Sk 2111) (Fig. 22)

Grave: N-S rectangular cut with rounded corners and a slightly rounded base. 1.8m x 0.5m, 0.11m deep.
Burial: slightly flexed, 70% complete, poor preservation, coffin nails.
Human Bone: adult female, 36-45 years, 154cm.
Pathology summary: caries, calculus, antemortem tooth loss, periodontal disease, DJD, trauma.
Dating: Romano-British pottery.

Fig. 22   Sk 2111 (grave 2110), looking east. Scale 1m

Grave 2113 (Sk 2115) (Fig. 23)

Grave: S-N sub-rectangular cut with squared corners and a flat base. 2.1m x 0.75m, 0.23m deep.
Burial: supine, 70% complete, moderate preservation, coffin nails.
Human Bone: adult female, 35-45 years, 158cm.
Pathology summary: caries, calculus, antemortem tooth loss, DJD, spinal DJD.
Grave Goods: hobnails.
Dating: Romano-British hobnails.

Fig. 23   Sk 2115 (grave 2113), looking west. Scales 1m, 1m and 0.3m

Pit 1600 (Sk 2135)

Grave: Circular pit with sloping sides and a concave base. 0.78m diameter, 0.15m deep.
Burial: disarticulated, 10% complete, very good preservation.
Human Bone: neonate, less than 1 month.
Dating: 2nd to 4th-century AD pottery.

Animal bone, by Jonny Geber

A total of 2189 fragments of animal bone, weighing 15kg, was analysed from Late Iron Age to Early Roman (Period 2) and Roman (Period 3) deposits (Table 5). The remains were generally poorly preserved and displayed a considerable degree of fragmentation. The material was subjected to a standard osteological analysis, and identified to species and element (Boessneck *et al.* 1964; Prummel and Frisch 1986; Schmid 1972; Iregren 2002). Estimation of age-at-death was conducted from epiphyseal fusion (Silver 1970) and dental attrition (Grant 1982; Vretemark 1997). Measurements were taken in accordance with von den Driesch (1976), and living shoulder heights were calculated following the formulae by Fock (1966) and Teichert (1975). A full tabulation of the results is available in the archive.

Period 2: Late Iron Age to Early Roman
Only a small quantity of bones was recovered from this period, and only those from pits 1052 and 1100 were identifiable to species. Pit 1052 contained four unburnt bone fragments identified as cattle and caprovine. The most substantial amount was present in pit 1100, which included fragments of five cattle bones, one horse tooth, one caprovine tibia, one burnt pig scapula fragment, and 12 unidentifiable mammal bones. Bones recovered from a brown rat and a common frog were very well preserved, and most likely represent modern animal burrowing when the field was used for market gardening.

Period 3: Roman
Bones (by weight) were predominately recovered from ditches (49.71%), layers (24.17%), pits (17.67%) and other features such as postholes, pits and rubble deposits (6.67%), as well as a small amount of bones from grave backfills (1.78%). A total of 146 fragments (140.29g) was burnt.

Species representation
Eight species were identified. Of the main domesticates, caprovine remains were most common by both fragment count (NISP) and minimum number of individuals (MNI), followed by cattle and pig (Table 5). When assessed by bone weight (BW), however, the dominance of cattle remains would suggest that beef was the primary protein source, followed by mutton and pork. Of the caprovine remains, nine bones could be identified as sheep *(Ovis aries)* and none as goat *(Capra hircus)*.

Much lesser quantities of other species were present in the material. Fifteen fragments were identified as horse, and eleven bones from birds, of which four could be identified as fowl. Wild species were represented by a left metatarsal and an antler fragment identified as red deer, and a hare bone. A quantity of rodent bones, as above, is likely to have been from recent animal burrowing.

Element representation
There was no predominance of particular elements observed in the bone material deriving from the meat-producing domesticates, and both meat-rich and meat-poor elements from the head, trunk, front, hind limbs and feet were present. It is therefore likely that the remains derive from the same limited number of animals that had been slaughtered on, or in close proximity to the site, as there was no noteworthy over- or under-representation of particular elements.

Table 5: Identified species by period, fragment count (NISP), minimum number of individuals (MNI) and bone weight (BW).
* = intrusive

| | Period 2 | | | | | | Period 3 | | | | | |
| | NISP | | MNI | | BW | | NISP | | MNI | | BW | |
	N	%	N	%	g	%	N	%	N	%	g	%
Cattle (Bos taurus)	7	14.29	2	28.57	418.53	81.15	273	12.76	6	18.18	7,803.70	54.24
Caprovine (Ovis aries/ Capra hircus)	2	4.08	1	14.29	3.42	0.66	431	20.14	18	54.55	2,636.99	18.33
Pig (Sus scrofa dom.)	1	2.04	1	14.29	8.54	1.66	36	1.68	4	12.12	447.41	3.11
Horse (Equus caballus)	1	2.04	1	14.29	38.20	7.41	15	0.70	1	3.03	826.70	5.75
Red deer (Cervus elaphus)	-	-	-	-	-	-	2	0.09	1	3.03	122.48	0.85
Brown hare (Lepus timidus)	-	-	-	-	-	-	1	0.05	1	3.03	1.31	0.01
Brown rat (Rattus norvegicus)*	13	26.53	1	14.29	0.11	0.02	-	-	-	-	-	-
Wood mouse (Apodemus sylvaticus)	-	-	-	-	-	-	21	0.98	1	3.03	0.23	< 0.00
Rodent (Rodentia sp.)*	3	6.12	-	-	0.02	< 0.00	21	0.98	-	-	0.15	< 0.00
Fowl (Gallus gallus)	-	-	-	-	-	-	4	0.19	1	3.03	3.46	0.02
Bird (Aves sp.)	-	-	-	-	-	-	7	0.33	-	-	1.12	0.01
Common frog (Rana temporaria)*	8	16.33	1	14.29	0.04	0.01	-	-	-	-	-	-
Large sized mammal	9	18.37	-	-	40.67	7.89	400	18.69	-	-	1,815.32	12.62
Medium sized mammal	3	6.12	-	-	5.04	0.98	551	25.75	-	-	546.97	3.80
Small sized mammal	-	-	-	-	-	-	2	0.09	-	-	0.99	0.01
Indeterminable	2	4.08	-	-	1.21	0.23	376	17.57	-	-	180.32	1.25
Total	49	100.00	7	100.00	515.78	100.00	2,140	100.00	33	100.00	14,387.15	100.00

Age and sex
The age estimations from the main domestic mammals revealed that the animals were primarily of mature age when slaughtered. Two cattle mandibles gave ages of 1–3 years (MWS = 25) and 4–8 years (MWS = 42), while the epiphyseal bone data (N = 29) indicated that most animals were slaughtered after the fourth year. Based on mandibles (N = 16), more than half of all caprovines were slaughtered between 4–6 years, while the epiphyseal bone data from the same species indicated that an initial slaughter period had also occurred between the first and second year. The pig epiphyseal bones indicate that they were primarily slaughtered between the first and third year, and one assessable mandible gave an age estimation of 2–5 years (MWS = 32).

There were only a few elements that could be sexed. Of the cattle remains, one coxae fragment was sexed as female and a metacarpal as male. The caprovine remains included a male astragalus and one coxae bone and two astragali from ewes. Of the pig remains, three canine teeth were sexed as boars, and one as sow.

Size
An estimation of living shoulder height could only be given from one cattle bone: a bull metacarpal (GL = 188.00mm), which indicated a height of 118cm. Shoulder heights in caprovine could be estimated from a radius (GL = 142.18mm) and a calcaneus (GL = 52.61mm), which gave statures of 57cm and 60cm.

Butchery
A few knife-cut marks were identified from the butchery process. Amongst the cattle remains, knife-cut marks were observed on the neck of a mandible, which is likely to relate to the removal of the head. A cervical vertebra indicated that the neck portion had been split axially, and fine knife-cut marks from filleting were observed on a rib and a radius bone. Caprovine remains revealed knife-cut marks on two proximal metapodials and one astragalus, which probably relate to the flaying/skinning process. Knives were also used when disarticulating the femora from the hip joints in two instances, and filleting knife-cut marks were observed on one rib fragment.

One horse bone, which was a shaft portion of a right metacarpal, displayed four transverse and parallel knife-cut marks across the postero-lateral portion of the distal end. These are likely to have been produced during flawing/skinning, and indicate that horsehides were utilized. There is no evidence that horse flesh was consumed.

Pathology
One cattle rib fragment, found in pit 1608, displayed a patch of very fine, active, and proliferated new bone formation on the visceral surface. This pathology indicates an inflammation of the periosteum, and is likely to relate to an active pulmonary infection at the time of slaughter of this animal.

Discussion
The small amount of bone from Period 2 deposits inhibits any comparison with the remains from the Period 3 contexts. Cattle, caprovine, pig and horse were all represented in both periods. From features dating to the Roman period, the animal bones indicate that a small amount of fowl, venison and hare also contributed to the diet. Overall, this species distribution is similar to that which has been noted in contemporaneous animal bone

assemblages from rural sites across Gloucestershire, such as Stoke Road, Bishop's Cleave (Maltby 2002); Frocester (Price 2000); Hucclecote (Stickler 2003); Haymes (Noddle 1986) and Thornhill Farm (Levine 2004). All these sites have indicated a livestock economy primarily based on caprovine and cattle, with little dependence on pigs and fowl. The assemblage suggests subsistence farming; the animals reared and butchered on, or close to the site, and all elements utilised.

The plant macrofossil and charcoal evidence, by Sarah Cobain

A total of 89 bulk soil samples was processed and assessed for plant macrofossil and charcoal remains. Sixteen of these samples containing quantities of well-preserved plant macrofossils and charcoal had the potential to provide additional information regarding the function of features sampled, socio-economic activities and to infer the composition of the local woodlands and flora, and these were selected for further analysis. The results are displayed in Tables 6 to 8.

Methodology
Plant macrofossil and charcoal remains were retrieved by standard flotation procedures. The seeds were identified with reference to Cappers *et al.* (2006), Berggren (1981) and Anderberg (1994). Up to 100 charcoal fragments (>2 mm) were identified with reference to Gale and Cutler (2000), Schoch *et al.* (2004) and Wheeler *et al.* (1989). Nomenclature of seeds and charcoal species follows Stace (1997). Full details of the methodologies are available in the archive.

Discussion
Period 2: Late Iron Age to Early Roman
Two samples from pit 1100 with a wide range of species were analysed (Table 6). Clay fragments recovered from the pit indicated that its contents may have been from an oven-type feature. The cereal-processing waste was dominated by spelt (*Triticum spelta*) with smaller amounts of oat (*Avena* spp), barley (*Hordeum vulgare*) and emmer (*Triticum dicoccum*). The spelt would have been used for producing bread. As no floret bases were identified, it was not possible to ascertain whether oat was cultivated or wild, but since the oat, along with barley, were present in small quantities, they were likely to be weed intrusions.

The presence of emmer wheat within this assemblage is of interest. Trends have shown that spelt dominated across central, southern and north-east England during the Iron Age. However in some assemblages, for example Cambourne, Cambridgeshire (Stevens 2009, 78–80) and Black Horse and Long Range, Devon (Clapham 1999a, 184–7; Clapham 1999b, 153), emmer wheat appears to have been of equal or greater importance as spelt, and it has been proposed that this may be the case in other areas of southern Britain (Campbell and Straker 2003, 18, 24). The small number of emmer grains amongst the processing waste in pit 1100 is suggestive of crop contamination rather than deliberate cultivation, although waste from a single pit may not be representative of the full range of crops grown or utilised at the site in this period.

A small amount of cereal chaff was also present within pit 1100. Using cereal processing waste to interpret crop processing stages is often problematic, as waste from an earlier

Table 6: *Plant macrofossil identifications.*

Habitat Preferences: A = arable used; D = weed indicative of disturbed areas; P = grassland/pasture weed; WL = marsh/wetland species; HSW = hedgerow/scrub/woodland species; E = economic species. All plants macrofossils are carbonised unless labelled (modern).

Period				2	2	3	3	3	3	3
Context number				1101	1139	1197	1200	1261	1332	1344
Feature number				1100	1100	1196	1199	Drying oven	Hollow J	Hollow J
Sample number (SS)				180	181	196	197	141	164	165
Flot volume (ml)				51.8	14	32.5	27	29	106.5	55
Sample volume (l)				34	15	34	30	30	38	34
Plant macrofossil preservation				Moderate	Good	Moderate	Moderate	Moderate	Moderate	Good
Habitat Code	**Family**	**Species**	**Common Name**							
HSW/WL	Adoxaceae	*Sambucus nigra*	Elder	cf 1	-	-	-	-	-	1
D/A	Amaranthaceae	*Chenopodium* spp	Fat hen/goosefoot spp	3	18	10	-	1	-	2
D/A		*Chenopodium* spp	Fat hen/goosefoot spp (modern)	17	18	-	4	-	23	2
A/D	Asteraceae	*Anthemis cotula*	Stinking chamomile	1	1	-	-	-	-	-
HSW	Betulaceae	*Corylus avellana*	Hazelnut	cf 1	-	1	cf 1	-	-	12
A/D	Brassicaceae	*Brassica* spp/*Sinapsis* spp	Mustard/cabbage/charlock	1	-	-	-	-	-	1
WL/D	Cyperaceae	*Carex* spp	Sedge	1	-	1	-	-	-	-
E	Fabaceae	*Pisum* spp	Pea spp	-	-	-	-	-	-	1
E		*Vicia faba*	Broad bean	-	-	-	cf 1	-	-	cf 1
A/P/D		*Vicia* spp/*Lathyrus* spp	Vetches/vetchlings (fragment)	-	-	1	1	-	-	-
A/P/D		*Vicia* spp/*Lathyrus* spp	Vetches/vetchlings (1-2mm) (half)	1	3	3	6	1	3	53
A/P/D		*Vicia* spp/*Lathyrus* spp	Vetches/vetchlings (1-2mm) (whole)	-	-	1	-	-	-	5
A/P/D		*Vicia* spp/*Lathyrus* spp	Vetches/vetchlings (2-3mm) (half)	2	-	3	3	-	-	8
A/P/D		*Vicia* spp/*Lathyrus* spp	Vetches/vetchlings (2-3mm) (whole)	-	-	-	1	-	-	2
E	Poaceae	*Avena* spp	Oat	13	12	-	1	4	-	-
E/A		*Avena* spp/*Bromus* spp	Oat/chess	3	1	-	-	1	-	-
A		*Bromus* spp	Chess	93	285	-	2	-	-	2
A/D		*Festuca* spp/*Lolium* spp	Festuce/rye grass	10	4	-	4	-	-	2
E		*Hordeum vulgare*	Hulled barley	26	9	cf 1	cf 2	2	cf 1	5

41

Table 6 (continued)

Habitat Code	Family	Species	Common Name	1101	1139	1197	1200	1261	1332	1344
			Period	2	2	3	3	3	3	3
			Context number	1101	1139	1197	1200	1261	1332	1344
			Feature number	1100	1100	1196	1199	drying oven	Hollow J	Hollow J
			Sample number (SS)	180	181	196	197	141	164	165
			Flot volume (ml)	51.8	14	32.5	27	29	106.5	55
			Sample volume (l)	34	15	34	30	30	38	34
			Plant macrofossil preservation	Moderate	Good	Moderate	Moderate	Moderate	Moderate	Good
E		*Hordeum vulgare*	6-row hulled barley	1	1	-	-	-	1	-
E		*Hordeum vulgare*	2-row hulled barley	-	1	-	-	-	-	-
E		*Hordeum vulgare*	Naked barley	-	1	-	-	1	-	1
E		*Triticum* spp	Wheat	12	10	-	-	7	-	1
E		*Triticum dicoccum*	Emmer	3	9	-	-	-	-	-
E		*Triticum spelta*	Spelt	247	458	-	-	47	2	11
E		*Triticum spelta*	Spelt glume bases	8	14	-	-	81	3	4
E		*Triticum dicoccum/spelta*	Emmer/spelt	9	6	-	-	3	-	1
E		*Triticum dicoccum/spelta*	Emmer/spelt glume bases	-	-	-	-	2	-	-
E		*Poaceae*	Indeterminate cereal grain	335	281	4	8	94	5	14
E		*Poaceae*	Culm node	2	-	-	-	-	1	-
E		*Poaceae*	Glume base	2	20	4	1	50	1	5
A/D/HSW	Polygonaceae	*Fallopia convolvulus*	Black-bindweed	4	1	-	-	-	-	-
A/D/WL		*Persicaria lapathifolia*	Pale persicaria	1	1	-	-	-	-	-
A/D/HSW		*Rumex* spp	Dock spp	26	9	-	-	4	-	10
HSW	Rosaceae	*Prunus spinosa*	Blackthorn/sloe	2	-	-	-	-	-	-
A/D	Rubiaceae	*Galium* spp	Cleavers/goosegrass	-	1	3	-	-	-	-
			Total	828	1165	31	35	299	39	143

Table 7: Plant macrofossil identifications
All plant macrofossils are carbonised unless otherwise indicated. For Habitat Codes see Table 6.

Period				3	3	3	3	3	
Context number				1406	1407	1417	1475	1566	
Feature number				1409	1409	Midden I	1474	1561	
Sample number (SS)				154	156	159	172	173	
Flot volume (ml)				11	13	34	59.2	25	
Sample volume (l)				8	8	28	30	8	
Plant macrofossil preservation				Moderate	Moderate	Moderate	Moderate	Moderate	
Habitat Code	**Family**	**Species**	**Common Name**						
D/A	Amaranthaceae	*Chenopodium* spp	Fat hen/goosefoot spp	1	-	-	-	-	
D/A		*Chenopodium* spp	Fat hen/goosefoot spp (modern)	-	-	39	4	-	
WL	Apiaceae	*Apium nodiflorum*	Fool's-water-cress	1	-	-	-	-	
A/D	Asteraceae	*Anthemis cotula*	Stinking chamomile	1	-	-	-	-	
HSW	Betulaceae	*Corylus avellana*	Hazelnut	2	-	23	2	3	
A/P/D	Fabaceae	*Vicia* spp/*Lathyrus* spp	Vetches/vetchlings (1-2mm) (half)	1	-	2	7	-	
A/P/D		*Vicia* spp/*Lathyrus* spp	Vetches/vetchlings (2-3mm) (half)	-	-	-	1	-	
E	Poaceae	*Avena* spp	Oat	-	-	1	1	-	
A		*Bromus* spp	Chess	-	-	-	3	-	
A/D		*Festuca* spp/*Lolium* spp	Festuce/rye grass	-	-	-	2	-	
E		*Hordeum vulgare*	Hulled barley	-	1	2	-	-	
E		*Triticum* spp	Wheat	-	1	1	2	1	
E		*Triticum spelta*	Spelt	-	-	-	2	1	
E		*Triticum spelta*	Spelt glume bases	-	-	-	7	-	
E		*Triticum dicoccum/spelta*	Emmer/spelt	1	1	1	-	1	
E		Poaceae	Indeterminate cereal grain	1	-	6	16	-	
E		Poaceae	Glume base	-	-	1	7	-	
E		Poaceae	Straw	-	-	1	-	-	
A/D/WL	Polygonaceae	*Persicaria lapathifolia*	Pale persicaria (modern)	1	-	1	-	-	
A/D/HSW		*Rumex* spp	Dock spp	1	-	-	3	-	
HSW	Rosaceae	*Crataegus monogyna*	Hawthorn	-	-	-	1	-	
A/D	Rubiaceae	*Galium* spp	Cleavers/goosegrass	1	-	-	1	-	
			Total	10	3	76	59	7	

stage may be burnt as fuel within a later processing stage. As a small amount of cereal chaff was present compared to grains within this assemblage, it is likely that the cereal crop had already been pounded and winnowed to release the cereal grains from their spikelets. The cereal chaff present may be remains from earlier pounding/winnowing stages being used as fuel. The carbonised cereal remains are most likely to represent accidental burning of grains which were being dried prior to storage or milling. This drying may have been carried out in the oven, of which fragments were found in pit 1100.

Weed seeds consisted of those indicative of an arable environment such as stinking chamomile (*Anthemis cotula*), cleavers/goosegrass (*Galium* spp), vetch/vetchlings (*Vicia/Lathyrus* spp) and chess (*Bromus* spp), and those of disturbed environments such as fat hen/goosefoot (*Chenopodium* spp), mustard/cabbage (*Brassica/Sinapsis* spp), dock (*Rumex* spp) and black-bindweed (*Fallopia convolvulus*). All these weeds grow to heights of up to half a metre or more (Stace 1997) indicating crops were harvested high up on the stems, with fewer low-growing weeds accidently included in the harvest. The presence of stinking chamomile implies a heavy clay soil (Stace 1997, 733). The small assemblage of vetch/vetchlings may simply have been weed intrusions, although with heavier clay soils present, they may have been deliberately cultivated to help fix nitrogen in the soil. Sedge (*Carex* spp) indicates marshland nearby, perhaps a waterlogged area of a field, or bordering the river Frome to the south. Blackthorn/sloe pips (*Prunus spinosa*) and hazelnut shells (*Corylus avellana*) may indicate gathering of wild food resources or may be from fruits/nuts attached to branches burnt as fuel.

Charcoal identified from pit 1100 consisted predominantly of hawthorn/rowan/crab apple (*Crataegus monogyna/Sorbus* spp/*Malus sylvestris*) and cherry (*Prunus* spp), with smaller amounts of elder (*Sambucus nigra*) and alder/hazel (*Alnus glutinosa/Corylus avellana*) (Table 8). Hawthorn/rowan/crab apple and cherry burn well but at lower temperatures than, for example, oak or ash (Gale and Cutler 2000, 120, 205). These species may have been selected as fuel for drying grain, which required low temperatures for short periods of time. These species are all indicative of scrub woodland/hedgerow from the local area. However, the small assemblage from a single feature does not necessarily contain a representative range of species present in local woodlands and used for fuel in this period.

Period 3: Roman
All plant remains analysed were from features associated with the enclosure. The largest assemblage of cereals was recovered from the drying oven. The remaining plant remains were represented as a homogeneous background scatter of plant remains from middens H and I, hollow J, and pits/ditches close to the midden deposits (Tables 6 and 7).

The cereal remains, which were dominated by spelt wheat with small numbers of oat and barley, are typical of those found in the Roman period (Cool 2006, 69) with the only change from the Period 2 pit assemblage being the absence of emmer wheat. Since oat and barley were recovered in small numbers, they are most likely weed intrusions. This type of assemblage has been identified at Frocester (Alvey *et al.* 2000, 257) and Horcott (Robinson 2004, 81). The spelt wheat would have been used to bake bread (Cool 2006, 70–1). Other deliberately cultivated crops include pea, broad bean and vetches. The vetch/vetchlings seeds may indicate a problem with soil fertility, with these grown on rotation to help improve the soil. Pea, broad bean and vetches were also known to have been used as vegetables or added to pottages and soups.

Table 8: Charcoal identifications

+ = 1-5 items; ++ = 6-20 items; +++ = 21-40 items; ++++ = >40 items
r/w = round wood
h/w = heartwood (tyloses present)

Family	Species	Common Name								
Period			2	3	3	3	3	3	3	3
Context number			1101	1200	1332	1344	1475	1500	1514	1566
Feature number			1100	1199	Hollow J	Hollow J	1474	1503	1513	1561
Sample number (SS)			182	197	164	165	172	166	174	173
Flot volume (ml)			35	27	106.5	55	59.2	103	20	25
Sample volume (l)			1	30	38	34	30	9	8	8
Charcoal quantity			++++	++ (s)	+++ (s)	++++ (s)	++++	++++	++++ (s)	+++
Charcoal preservation			Good	Moderate	Moderate	Moderate	Moderate	Good	Moderate	Moderate
Adoxaceae	*Sambucus nigra*	Elder	4	-	-	-	-	-	-	-
Betulaceae	*Alnus glutinosa/Corylus avellana*	Alder/hazel	1	1	7	11	-	9	4	5
	Betula spp	Birch r/w	-	-	2	-	-	-	-	-
	Corylus avellana	Hazel r/w	-	-	-	-	2	-	-	4
Fabaceae	*Ulex* spp/*Cytisus* spp	Gorse/Broom r/w	-	-	-	-	2	-	-	-
Fagaceae	*Quercus robur/petraea*	Sessile/pedunculate oak	-	3	2	5	6	13	5	5
	Quercus robur/petraea hw	Sessile/pedunculate oak h/w	-	-	1	-	-	2	-	4
Oleaceae	*Fraxinus excelsior*	Ash	-	7	3	5	9	-	3	6
Rosaceae	*Crataegus monogyna/Sorbus* spp/*Malus sylvestris*	Hawthorn/rowan/crab apple	11	3	9	5	10	6	7	5
	Crataegus monogyna/Sorbus spp/*Malus sylvestris*	Hawthorn/rowan/crab apple r/w	-	-	-	1	-	-	-	-
	Prunus spp	Cherry spp	14	-	2	1	-	-	1	1
Ulmaceae	*Ulmus glabra*	Elm	-	-	-	-	1	-	-	-
		Indeterminate	-	5	4	-	-	-	5	-
		Total	30	14	26	28	30	30	20	30

Cereal chaff was only recovered in any volume from Roman features from the drying oven, where the quantities suggest cereal processing was being carried out, but it is difficult to ascertain which stage of cereal processing is represented. This assemblage exhibits a higher ratio of glume bases to cereal grains than from pit 1100 from the earlier period. It is possible that the pounded grain was being dried prior to storage/milling and the pounding/threshing waste was being used as fuel within the stoking pit (van der Veen 1989, 303). Alternatively, the cereal crop was being parched in the drying oven to make the spikelets more brittle (thereby easier to separate the grains) prior to pounding/winnowing, and some grains and glumes accidently became carbonised. The chaff present in small amounts in other midden/pit deposits is likely to be either firing debris waste from the drying oven or perhaps chaff used as kindling in other fires on site.

The small number of weed seeds suggests the grain spikelets were stored or brought to the site clean. Arable weeds such as cleavers/goosegrass spp, chess, vetch/vetchlings and stinking chamomile are present, and species indicative of a disturbed environment such as fat hen, mustard/cabbage and dock were identified. As with the Period 2 assemblage, all these species typically reach half a metre or more in height, again suggesting crops were harvested high on the stems. Fool's-watercress and sedge identified are indicative of marshland environments nearby. An elder seed, hawthorn pip and hazelnut shell indicate wild foodstuffs available in the local area, either deliberately gathered, or attached to branches burnt as fuel.

Fuel sources represented by firing debris within middens, pits and ditches consisted predominantly of oak, ash and hawthorn/rowan/crab apple with smaller amounts of alder/hazel and occasional elder, birch (*Betula* spp), hazel, gorse/broom (*Ulex* spp/*Cytisus* spp), cherry spp and elm (*Ulmus glabra*) (Table 8). This assemblage differs from Period 2 pit 1100 in that a wider range of species are represented including oak and ash, although this may be a reflection of the larger number of analysed samples. The presence of oak and ash suggests fuel was being sought for industrial processes (e.g. metalworking), or perhaps larger-scale cereal processing where long-lasting fuels were required.

DISCUSSION
by Neil Holbrook

Human activity at Foxes Field can be traced back as far as the Mesolithic period, evidenced by the recovery of two diagnostically Mesolithic flint artefacts, including part of an adze. Early Neolithic activity is identified solely by a leaf-shaped flint arrowhead, although some of the other flint blades and flakes may also date to this period. All of these finds occurred as residual material in later features. The earliest stratified evidence comprised Beaker pottery sherds and worked flints from tree-throw pit 1005. This isolated pit provides another example of how commercial archaeological work ostensibly focussed on sites of later periods is revealing these kinds of features in increasing numbers in western Britain. Darvill (2006, 29–30) discusses recent Gloucestershire finds of Beaker material, including the recovery of small amounts of Beaker pottery in colluvium overlying a late 2nd millennium BC old ground surface at The Buckles, Frocester, 3.5km to the south-west of the site (Price 2000, 204); Mullin (2011, 101–2) provides some further examples from Gloucestershire. Another recent discovery is an isolated pit with pottery and flint at Staverton, North Wiltshire (Barber *et al.* 2013, 18). Beaker occupation sites with structural remains continue to remain elusive, however.

The next period of activity recorded at Foxes Field (Period 2) comprised a small number of small pits which yielded Late Iron Age or Early Roman pottery. These were found scattered across the area subsequently occupied by the Romano-British enclosure. The majority of the pottery recovered from these features is of Malvernian origin, which is often chronologically undiagnostic (unfeatured sherds could date anywhere between the 4th century BC and 1st century AD). If the pits do relate to a single coherent phase of activity this is most likely to date to the mid 1st century AD, to judge by the presence of sherds from a collared flagon of this date from pit 1388 in the southern part of the site. The flagon came from the fill of a pit which also contained the base of a large storage jar set upright on its base; two other examples of this practice were also found (1369 and 1391). In all three cases the pits were just large enough to hold the vessels set upright within them. There was no evidence to suggest that they were cremation urns. Similar deposits were found at Frocester Court where the bases of four large Malvernian jars had been placed upright in small holes: just inside roundhouse 4 (Mid-Late Iron Age); just outside roundhouse 6 (Late Iron Age) and two vessels associated with rectangular building B1 (2nd century AD) (Price 2000, 51, 58, 72, fig. 9.3, 60). These vessels might have been used for some form of cold storage, unless they were ritually-inspired depositions. The latter interpretation appears more plausible for the vessels recovered from the Late Iron Age and Roman farmstead at New Moreton Farm, Standish, 4.5km to the north-west. Here a stack of Late Iron Age/Early Roman coarseware jars were cut into a silted-up gully that probably surrounded a roundhouse (WA 2004, 9–10, 13).

Another Period 2 pit (1100) at Foxes Field contained a quantity of spelt wheat and the fired-clay remains of a probable oven, testifying to the processing of crops nearby, and by inference, settlement not too far distant. Given that settlement would have avoided areas susceptible to flooding, its most likely location is just to the south of the excavated area, between the B4008 and the north bank of the Frome.

The next phase of activity is represented by the establishment of the enclosure, and there is no reason to assume any chronological break between Periods 2 and 3. It is conceivable that the plan of the enclosure as revealed in the excavation developed over time rather than being created in a single operation, if the differing dates for the pottery groups recovered from the fills of the enclosure ditches are not just the product of differential degrees of later recutting. Based upon the pottery the earliest ditches to be filled were B and D. Ditch B was aligned north-south and established the eastern side of the enclosure and the alignment of trackway L, which presumably served as a droveway leading out onto the hill pasture of Doverow Hill to the north. The east/west Ditches A, 1446 and F were perhaps primarily dug to catch and channel surface water running down the slope. The enclosure appears to have been open on its western side, unless it was defined by a bank, hedge or fence, which left no trace. If this formed a continuation of upcast banks on the inner lips of Ditches A and D then it would have cut across gully O (which may mark the site of a building) and would place circular structure K outside of the enclosure. Neither feature is well dated and they could relate to Period 2. There is no compulsion or necessity to envisage an enclosure defined on all four sides. Three-sided enclosures are by no means unknown in the Late Iron Age and Romano-British countryside, as for instance at Groundwell West, Swindon, Enclosure E1 (Walker *et al.* 2001). Ditches C and E most probably defined internal divisions. The features associated with the enclosure do not make for easy interpretation – most are isolated pits and postholes. Nevertheless it is reasonable to assume that there were a number of structures within the excavated area, although only a few could be recognised with any degree of confidence. Structures formed from surface-laid timber beams or cob are both possible. Circular post-built structure K was only 6m in diameter, small for a domestic roundhouse, although a shepherd's hut or breeding pen are possible interpretations. There are also suggestions of another circular structure, approximately 5m in diameter, associated with scorched pit 1383. Gully O might define the site of a rectangular building, the gully only being required on the up-slope side to catch run off. L-shaped feature 1307 might also conceivably have formed a rubble foundation for a cob building. Refuse from activity within the enclosure or from the core settlement nearby was deposited in middens H and I, both of which contained plant remains although H yielded considerably more pottery than I. Such middens survive only rarely on plough-damaged sites, although local examples include Hucclecote and Weaver's Bridge, Cricklade (Thomas *et al.* 2003; Mudd *et al.* 1999, 148–50).

Overall it would appear that the establishment of the enclosure dates to the late 1st or early 2nd century AD and that the ditches had either largely silted-up or been deliberately infilled by the end of the 2nd century AD. This reorganisation might be a reflection of changes in the core of the settlement itself. The recovery of fragments of box flue tile in a 4th-century AD deposit indicates that by that time there was a high-status building in the vicinity equipped with a hypocaust. This building might also have been the source of the fragments of building stone and pennant sandstone roof tile, and the lead setting for a samian tessera, recovered from late Roman contexts. In the context of rural Gloucestershire it is reasonable to infer that a villa house was added to a pre-existing farmstead sometime in the 3rd or 4th century AD, as at Frocester Court where the villa house dates to *c.* AD 275. Foxes Field may therefore be added to the other known villas in this stretch of the Frome valley. To the west a villa is known at Whitminster (Scott 1993, GS 105; Chouls 1977, 23); to the north-east one is suspected from chance finds at Cashes Green, Stroud (Scott 1993, GS 92; Gracie 1968, 204) and to the east near Stroud Vicarage (Scott 1993, GS 93; Young 1977b, 30). On the south side of the Frome there are further sites at Kings Stanley

(Scott 1993, GS 62/3; Heighway 1989); Frocester Court (Scott 1993, GS 50) and Frocester St Peter (Gracie 1963; Price 2000, 223–32). Only Frocester Court is known in any detail.

Later activity within the excavated area was of a somewhat different character to that which had gone before and comprised a T-shaped drying oven, an eroded hollow (J) and human burial. The oven is only dated by a few sherds of 3rd or 4th-century AD pottery from its demolition. It is conceivable therefore that it dates to the 2nd century AD along with the other agricultural activity within the enclosure, although it could be later. Such ovens are a regular occurrence on Romano-British rural settlements in central/southern Britain; where dated the majority are of a 3rd or 4th-century AD date (Morris 1979, table 1). Hollow J was most likely an eroded hollow-way leading southwards towards the main area of settlement. It seemingly possessed a crude surface formed form iron-working slag. Close to the hollow-way was unusual pit 2120, which may be regarded as an example of structured deposition given the recovery of a complete quern stone, a blade from an iron shears and a Dobunnic silver coin that had been curated for several centuries, amongst other finds.

To judge from the slag recovered, especially from hollow J, iron-making contributed to the economy of the settlement. Possible unused iron ore in the form of iron-rich stone was also recovered from pit 1725 to the east of the hollow J. The slag indicates that both smelting and smithing took place, and some of the smelting was seemingly more in keeping with Late Iron Age metallurgical practices than that more usually attested in the Roman period, although this observation need not necessarily indicate that any of the smelting occurred before the mid 1st century AD. Iron-making was a common activity at rural sites on the reclaimed alluvial land along the Cotswold bank of the Severn Estuary, and Foxes Field now provides another example of the contribution that iron-making made to the rural economy (Allen and Fulford 1987). Further evidence for metalworking has recently been discovered *c.* 2.2km to the west on land south of the Bristol Road, Stonehouse. Here, geophysical survey and evaluation trenches revealed a similar pattern of enclosure ditches and a possible trackway aligned towards the River Frome. Provisional interpretation of the archaeological remains suggests activity on the southern periphery of settlement including small-scale industry, focussed in the 1st to 2nd century AD, and extending into the 3rd century AD (OA 2013). Although there appear to be some similarities between the sites in terms of date, location and character, the Bristol Road site lacks evidence for either higher-status buildings in the vicinity, or for use of the site into the 4th century AD, which are both present at Foxes Field.

The fourteen inhumation burials found across the enclosure area all apparently date to the later Roman period. In addition, disarticulated bones from a neonate were recovered from pit 1600. There is no obvious patterning to grave position, orientation or mode of burial. Grave 1192 contained the bodies of a mature male and female closely flexed together, indicating a close bond between two people who presumably died at the same time (Fig. 6). One mature male in grave 1193 was buried in the prone position with hobnailed footware and a coin of AD 324–30 found adjacent to the mouth. A mature female (grave 1171) was buried in a flexed position with an iron cleaver next to her upper right arm. This is not a common Romano-British practice; most of the other known examples date to the Late Roman period (Philpott 1991, 176–7). There was only one instance of intercutting burials: the grave of a child of 6–12 years of age and of indeterminate sex (1167) cut into the backfill of that of a female of 26–35 years of age (1217). It is entirely plausible that these two individuals were mother and child.

Scattered burials are now recognised as a typical facet of many Romano-British rural settlements, and their presence at Foxes Field occasions little surprise (Thomas *et al.* 2003, 64–5). Comparison with the burials at Frocester Court is instructive, as there is a very different demographic profile at the two sites. Of the fifteen burials at Foxes Field one was a neonate; one a child of around ten and the remainder adults, of which seven were sexed as female and five male. At Frocester Court 69 burials were found, of which 66 were inhumations and three cremations (Price 2000; 2010). Forty were perinatal infants and 27 children or adults. The lack of perinatal infants at Foxes Field compared to Frocester Court is evident, and both sites show an absence of 1st or 2nd-century AD cremations, which is widely assumed to have been the prevalent burial rite at this time. Perhaps the absence of perinatal infants at Foxes Field is a product of the peripheral location of the excavation area to the main settlement; if that were available for investigation a different pattern might be revealed.

There is little reliable evidence from the excavation upon which to infer how long the settlement continued in use. The latest of the three Roman coins dated to AD 353–54 and shell-tempered ware, which occurs on sites occupied in the second half of the 4th century AD, is absent. It is far from certain, however, whether such a pattern would hold true if the settlement itself was investigated, and so it is best for now to defer judgement on this issue.

ACKNOWLEDGEMENTS

Cotswold Archaeology would like to thank Barratt Homes (Bristol), and in particular John Drew, Technical Project Manager, for supporting this project. Thanks also go to Charles Parry, Senior Archaeological Officer, Gloucestershire County Council, who monitored the fieldwork and post-excavation. The fieldwork was managed by Simon Cox, and was directed by Mark Brett. Post-excavation work was managed by Mary Alexander. The illustrations are by Daniel Bashford, Lorna Gray and Peter Moore. The site archive will be deposited with The Museum in the Park, Stroud, under accession number STGCM 2010.65.

BIBLIOGRAPHY

Primary Sources

GRO (Gloucestershire Archives):
   GRO/P316a SD2 1839 Tithe Map of Stonehouse, Gloucestershire
   GRO/GDR/T1/146 1842 Tithe Map of Randwick, Gloucestershire

*NMR (***National Monuments Record - Aerial Photographs***)*
   NMR 216, RAF/3G/TUD/UK/102, Frame V5005, 30-Mar-46. 1 A 10000 12 BW87
      MOD RAF
   NMR 1102, RAF/58/503, Frame V5067, 11-Jun-50. 1 A 6500 10 BW87 MOD RAF
   NMR 9399, OS/68298, Frame V9 P 07-Sep-68. 1 A 7500 12 BW99 NMR CRW
   NMR 10196, OS/71071, Frame V156, 12-Apr-71. 1 A 7000 12 BW99 NMR CRW

Secondary Sources

Allen, J.R.L. and Fulford, M.G. 1987 'Romano-British settlement and industry on the wetlands of the Severn estuary', *Antiq. J.* **67**, 237–89

Allen J.R.L. and Scott A.C. (forthcoming) 'The whetstone blanks from the Forum gutter at Roman Wroxeter: the case for provenance', *Shropshire Hist. Archaeol.*

Alvey, R.C., Clark, H.H. and Ede, J.E. 2000 'Plant remains', in E. Price 2000, 253–8

Anderberg, A.-L. 1994 *Atlas of seeds, Part 4* Uddevalla, Swedish Museum of Natural History

Antiquaries Journal 1927 'Notes: Roman iron from Cirencester', *Antiq. J.* **7**, 320–1

Arthur, P. 1978 'The Lead Glazed wares of Roman Britain', in P. Arthur and G. Marsh (eds) 1978, *Early Finewares in Roman Britain* BAR Brit. Ser. **57**, Oxford, British Archaeological Reports, 293–353

Aufderheide, A.C. and Rodríguez-Martín, C. 1998 *The Cambridge encyclopedia of human paleopathology* Cambridge, Cambridge University Press

Ayoub, A. 2010 'Dentofacial infection', in L. Andersson, K.-E. Kahnberg and M.A. Pogrel (eds) 2010, *Oral and maxillofacial surgery* Oxford, Wiley-Blackwell, 125–36

Barber, A., Schuster, J. and Holbrook, N. 2013 'Prehistoric activity and Roman rural settlement at Blacklands, Staverton: excavations in 2007', *Wilts. Archaeol. Natur. Hist. Mag.* **106**, 16–51

Berggren, G. 1981 *Atlas of seeds, Part 3* Arlöv, Swedish Museum of Natural History

Boessneck, J., Müller, H.-H. and Teichert, M. 1964 'Osteologische Unterscheidungsmerkmale zwischen Schaf (*Ovis aries* Linné) und Ziege (*Capra hircus* Linné)', *Kühn-Archiv* **78** (1–2), 1–129

Boocock, P., Roberts, C.A. and Manchester, K. 1995 'Maxillary sinusitis in medieval Chichester, England', *American J. Physical Anthropol.* **98** (4), 483–95

Brickley, M. and McKinley, J.I. (eds) 2004 *Guidelines to the standards for recording human remains* IFA Papers **7**, Reading, IFA/BABAO

Brickley, M. and Ives, R. 2008 *The bioarchaeology of metabolic disease* Amsterdam, Academic Press

BGS (British Geological Survey) 1975 *1:50,000 Geological Survey of Great Britain (England and Wales), Solid and Drift, map sheet 234: Gloucester* Keyworth, British Geological Survey

Buikstra, J.E. and Ubelaker, D.H. (eds) 1994 *Standards for data collection from human skeletal remains*, Arkansas Archeol. Survey Res. Ser. **44**, Fayetteville, Arkansas Archeological Survey

Butterworth, C.A., Fitzpatrick, A.P. and Grove, J. 1999 *Prehistoric and Roman sites in East Devon: the Honiton to Exeter Improvement DBFO Scheme, 1996–9, Volume 1* Salisbury, Trust for Wessex Archaeology

Campbell, G. and Straker, V. 2003 'Prehistoric crop husbandry and plant use in southern England: development and regionality', in K.A. Robson Brown (ed.) 2003, *Archaeological Sciences 1999: Proceedings of the Archaeological Sciences Conference, University of Bristol, 1999* BAR Int. Ser. **1111**, Oxford, Archaeopress, 14–30

Cappers, R.T.J., Bekker, R.M. and Jans, J.E.A. 2006 *Digital seed atlas of the Netherlands* Groningen Archaeological Studies **4**, Eelde, Barkhuis Publishing www.seedatlas.nl (accessed February/March 2013)

Case, H. 1993 'Beakers: Deconstruction and After', *Proc. Prehist. Soc.* **59**, 241–68

Chouls, W. 1977 'Site Reports: Eastington, Whitminster Roman Villa', *Glevensis* **11**, 23

Clapham, A.J. 1999a 'Charred plant remains', in C.A. Butterworth, A.P. Fitzpatrick and J. Grove 1999, 184–8

Clapham, A.J. 1999b 'Charred plant remains', in C.A. Butterworth, A.P. Fitzpatrick and J. Grove 1999, 152–5

Cool, H.E.M. 2006 *Eating and Drinking in Roman Britain* Cambridge, Cambridge University Press

Dar, G., Masharawi, Y., Peleg, S., Steinberg, N., May, H., Medlej, B., Peled, N. and Hershkovitz, I. 2010 'Schmorl's nodes distribution in the human spine and its possible etiology', *European Spine J.* **19** (4), 670–5

Darvill, T. 1984 'Neolithic Gloucestershire', in A. Saville (ed.) 1984, *Archaeology in Gloucestershire* Cheltenham, Cheltenham Art Gallery/Bristol and Gloucestershire Archaeological Society, 81–112

Darvill, T. 2006 'Early Prehistory', in N. Holbrook and J. Juřica (eds) 2006, *Twenty-five years of archaeology in Gloucestershire: a review of new discoveries and new thinking in Gloucestershire, South Gloucestershire and Bristol 1979–2004* Bristol Gloucestershire Archaeol. Rep. **3**, Cirencester, Cotswold Archaeology, 5–60

Dearne, M.J. and Branigan, K. 1995 'The use of coal in Roman Britain', *Antiq. J.* **75**, 71–105

Dias, G.J. and Tayles, N. 1997 "Abscess cavity' – a misnomer', *Int. J. Osteoarchaeol.* **7** (5), 548–54

Dias, G.J., Prasad, K. and Santos, A.L. 2007 'Pathogenesis of apical periodontal cysts: guidelines for diagnosis in palaeopathology', *Int. J. Osteoarchaeol.* **17** (6), 619–26

Ellis, P. 1987 'Sea Mills, Bristol: the 1965-1968 excavations in the Roman town of Abonae', *Trans Bristol Gloucestershire Archaeol. Soc.* **105**, 15–108

Eckardt, H. and Crummy, N. 2008 *Styling the body in Late Iron Age and Roman Britain: a contextual approach to toilet implements* Monographies Instrumentum **36**, Montagnac, Éditions Monique Mergoil

Etheridge, D. 2008 'Fox's Field, Ebley Road, Stonehouse, Gloucestershire: Archaeological Desk Based Assessment', unpublished Avon Archaeological Unit report

Faccia, K.J. and Williams, R.C. 2008 'Schmorl's nodes: Clinical significance and implications for the bioarchaeological record', *Int. J. Osteoarchaeol.* **18** (1), 28–44

Ferembach, D., Schwidetzky, I. and Stloukal, M. 1980 'Recommendations for age and sex diagnoses of skeletons', *J. Hum. Evol.* **9** (1), 517–49

Flohr, S. and Schultz, M. 2009a 'Mastoiditis – paleopathological evidence of a rarely reported disease', *American J. Physical Anthropol.* **138** (3), 266–73

Flohr, S., and Schultz, M. 2009b 'Osseous changes due to mastoiditis in human skeletal remains', *Int. J. Osteoarchaeol.* **19** (1), 99–106

Fock, J. 1966 'Metrische Untersuchungen an Metapodien einiger europäischer Rinderrassen', unpublished dissertation, Munich, Universität München

Gale, R. and Cutler, D.F. 2000 *Plants in Archaeology, Identification Manual of Artefacts of Plant Origin from Europe and the Mediterranean* Otley, Westbury and the Royal Botanic Gardens Kew

Geber, J. and Murphy, E. 2012 'Scurvy in the Great Irish Famine: Evidence of vitamin C deficiency from a mid-19th century skeletal population', *American J. Physical Anthropol.* **148** (4), 512–24

GeoQuest 2009 'Geophysical Survey of Foxes Field, North Side of Ebley Road, Stonehouse, Gloucestershire', in Young 2009a (unpublished report)

Gibson, A.M. 1982 *Beaker Domestic Sites* BAR Brit. Ser. **107**, Oxford, British Archaeological Reports

Gracie, H. 1963 'St Peter's church, Frocester', *Trans Bristol Gloucestershire Archaeol. Soc.* **82**, 148–67

Gracie, H. 1968 'Some new Romano-British sites in Gloucestershire', *Trans Bristol Gloucestershire Archaeol. Soc.* **87**, 202–5

Grant, A. 1982 'The use of tooth wear as a guide to the age of domestic ungulates', in B. Wilson, C. Grigson and S. Payne (eds) 1982, *Ageing and sexing animal bones from archaeological sites* BAR Brit. Ser. **109**, Oxford, British Archaeological Reports, 91–108

Heighway, C. 1989 'Excavations near the site of St George's church, King's Stanley', *Glevensis* **23**, 33–42

Henig, M. 1978 *A corpus of Roman engraved gemstones from British sites* BAR Brit. Ser. **8**, Oxford, British Archaeological Reports

Hillson, S. 2005 *Teeth* Cambridge, Cambridge University Press

Iregren, E. 2002 *Bildkompendium: Historisk osteologi* Dept Archaeol. Ancient Hist. Rep. Ser. **85**, Lund, University of Lund

Johns, C. 1996 *The Jewellery of Roman Britain* London, University College London

Kelley, M.A. 1982 'Intervertebral osteochondrosis in ancient and modern populations', *American J. Physical Anthropol.* **59** (3), 271–9

Kelley, M.A. and Micozzi, M.S. 1984 'Rib lesions in chronic pulmonary tuberculosis', *American J. Physical Anthropol.* **65** (4), 381–6

Kinnes, I., Gibson, A., Bowman, S., Leese, M. and Boast, R. 1991 'Radiocarbon dating and British Beakers: The British Museum Programme', *Scottish Archaeol. Rev.* **8**, 35–84

Kirk, J.R. 1949 'Bronzes from Woodeaton, Oxon', *Oxoniensia* **14**, 1–45

Kudo, S., Minuro, O. and Russell, W.J. 1983 'Ossification of thoracic ligamenta flava', *American J. Roentgenol.* **141** (1), 117–21

Lambert, P.M. 2002 'Rib lesions in a prehistoric Puebloan sample from southwestern Colorado', *American J. Physical Anthropol.* **117** (4), 282–92

Levine, M. 2004 'The faunal remains', in D. Jennings, J. Muir, S. Palmer and A. Smith, *Thorhill Farm, Fairford, Gloucestershire: An Iron Age and Roman pastoral site in the Upper Thames Valley* Thames Valley Landscapes Monograph **23**, Oxford, Oxford Archaeology, 109–33

Lewis, M.E., Roberts, C.A. and Manchester, K. 1995 'Comparative study of the prevalence of maxillary sinusitis in later medieval urban and rural populations in northern England', *American J. Physical Anthropol.* **98** (4), 497–506

Mack, R.P. 1975 *The Coinage of Ancient Britain* London, Spink and Son

Mackreth, D. 2011 *Brooches in Late Iron Age and Roman Britain* Oxford, Oxbow Books

Maltby, M. 2002 'The animal bone', in D. Enright and M. Watts 2002, *A Romano-British and medieval settlement site at Stoke Road, Bishop's Cleeve, Gloucestershire* Bristol Gloucestershire Archaeol. Rep. **1**, Cirencester, Cotswold Archaeology, 44–9

Manning, W.H. 1985 *Catalogue of the Romano-British Iron Tools, Fittings and Weapons in the British Museum* London, British Museum

Matos, V. and Santons, A.L. 2006 'On the trail of pulmonary tuberculosis based on rib lesions: results from the human identified skeletal collection from the Museu Bocage (Lisbon, Portugal)', *American J. Physical Anthropol.* **130** (2), 190–200

Mays, S., Fysh, E. and Taylor, G.M. 2002 'Investigation of the link between visceral surface rib lesions and tuberculosis in a medieval skeletal series from England using ancient DNA', *American J. Physical Anthropol.* **119** (1), 27–36

Morris, P. 1979 *Agricultural Buildings in Roman Britain* BAR Brit. Ser. **70**, Oxford, British Archaeological Reports

Mudd, A., Williams, R.J. and Lupton, A. 1999 *Excavations alongside Roman Ermin Street, Gloucestershire and Wiltshire: the archaeology of the A419/417 Swindon to Gloucester Road Scheme. Vol. 1: Prehistoric and Roman activity* Oxford, Oxford Archaeological Unit

Mullin, D. 2011 'Neolithic to Bronze Age', in E. Biddulph and K. Welsh, *Cirencester before Corinium* Thames Valley Landscapes **34**, Oxford, Oxford Archaeology, 97–102

Nijs, S. and Broos, P.L.O. 2004 'Fractures of the distal radius: A contemporary approach', *Acta chirurgica Belgica* **104** (4), 401–12

Noddle, B. 1986 'The animal bones', in B. Rawes, 'The Romano-British settlement at Haymes, Cleeve Hill, near Cheltenham', *Trans. Bristol Gloucestershire Archaeol. Soc.* **104**, 61–93

OA (Oxford Archaeology) 2013 'Land to the South of Bristol Road, Stonehouse, Gloucestershire: Archaeological Evaluation Report', unpublished Oxford Archaeology South report **5648**

Ortner, D.J. 2003 *Identification of pathological conditions in human skeletal remains* London, Academic Press

Oxenham, M.F. and Cavill, I. 2010 'Porotic hyperostosis and cribra orbitalia. The erythropoietic response to iron-deficiency anaemia', *Anthropol. Sci.* **118** (3), 199–200

Paynter S. 2006 'Regional variations in bloomery smelting slag of the Iron Age and Romano-British periods', *Archaeometry* **48** (2), 271–92

Paynter S. 2007 'Innovations in bloomery smelting in Iron Age and Romano-British England', in S. La Niece, D. Hook, and P. Craddock (eds.) 2007, *Metals and Mines: Studies in Archaeometallurgy* London, Archetype

Philpott, R. 1991 *Burial practices in Roman Britain: a survey of grave treatment and furnishing AD 43–410* BAR Brit. Ser. **219**, Oxford, British Archaeological Reports

Price, E. 2000 *Frocester: a Romano-British Settlement, its antecedents and successors, Volume 2, The Finds* Stonehouse, Gloucester and District Archaeological Research Group

Price, E. 2010 *Frocester: a Romano-British Settlement, its antecedents and successors, Volume 3, Excavations 1995–2009* Stonehouse, Gloucester and District Archaeological Research Group

Prummel, W. and Frisch, H.J. 1986 'A guide for the distinction of species, sex and body side in bones of sheep and goat', *J. Archaeol. Sci.* **13**, 567–77

Rigby, V. 1982a 'The Coarse Pottery', in J. Wacher and A. McWhirr 1982, *Cirencester Excavations I: Early Roman Occupation at Cirencester* Gloucester, Cirencester Excavation Committee/Alan Sutton, 153–204

Rigby, V. 1982b 'The Coarse Pottery', in A. McWhirr, L. Viner and C. Wells 1982, *Cirencester Excavations Volume II: Romano-British Cemeteries at Cirencester* Gloucester, Cirencester Excavation Committee/Alan Sutton, Microfiche Section C13–D10

Roberts, C.A. 2007 'A bioarchaeological study of maxillary sinusitis', *American J. Physical Anthropol.* **133** (2), 792–807

Roberts, C.A. and Cox, M. 2003 *Health and disease in Britain: From prehistory to the present day* Stroud, Sutton Publishing

Roberts, C.A. and Manchester, K. 2005 *The archaeology of disease* Stroud, Sutton Publishing

Robinson, M. 2004 'Macroscopic plant and invertebrate remains', in J. Pine and S. Preston 2004, *Iron Age and Roman settlement and landscape at Totterdown Lane, Horcott, near Fairford, Gloucestershire, Reading* TVAS Monograph **6**, Reading, Thames Valley Archaeological Services, 81–7

Roe F. 1979 'Typology of stone implements with shaftholes', in T.H.M. Clough and W.A. Cummins (eds) 1979, *Stone Axe Studies: Archaeological, Petrological, Experimental and Ethnographic*, 23–48

Roe, F. 2007 'Worked stone', in D. Miles, S. Palmer, A. Smith and G. Perpetua Jones 2007, *Iron Age and Roman Settlement in the Upper Thames Valley: Excavations at Claydon Pike and other sites within the Cotswold Water Park* Thames Valley Landscapes **26**, Oxford, Oxford Archaeology, 144–150 and 193–4

Rogers, J., Watt, I. and Dieppe, P. 1985 'Palaeopathology of spinal ostephytosis, vertebral ankylosis, ankylosing spondylitis, and vertebral hyperostosis', *Annals Rheumatic Diseases* **44** (2), 113–20

Rogers, J., Waldron, T., Dieppe, P. and Watt, I. 1987 'Arthopathies in palaeopathology: the basis of classification according to most probable cause', *J.Archaeol. Sci.* **14** (2), 179–93

Saluja, G., Fitzpatrick, K., Bruce, M. and Cross, J. 1986 'Schmorl's nodes (intravertebral herniations of intervertebral disc tissue) in two historic British populations', *J. Anatomy* **145**, 87–96

Schmid, E. 1972 *Atlas of animal bones: For prehistorians, archaeologists and quaternary geologists* Amsterdam, Elsevier Publishing Company

Schoch, W., Heller, I., Schweingruber, F. H. and Kienast, F. 2004 *Wood anatomy of Central European species* www.woodanatomy.ch (accessed February/March 2013)

Scott, E. 1993 *A gazetteer of Roman villas in Britain* Leicester Archaeol. Monograph **1**, Leicester, University of Leicester

Scott, I. 1998 'Iron hobnails and other shoe fittings', in J. Timby 1998, *Excavations at Kingscote and Wycombe, Gloucestershire* Cirencester, Cotswold Archaeological Trust, 165

Shaffrey, R. 2006 *Grinding and Milling: A Study of Romano-British rotary querns and millstones made from Old Red Sandstone* BAR Brit. Ser. **409**, Oxford, British Archaeological Reports

Seager-Smith, R. and Davies, S.M. 1993 'Roman pottery', in P.J. Woodward, S.M. Davies and A.H. Graham 1993, *Excavations at Greyhound Yard, Dorchester 1981–4* Dorset Nat. Hist. Archaeol. Soc. Monograph **12**, Dorchester, Dorset Natural History and Archaeological Society, 202–84

Silver, I.A. 1970 'The ageing of domestic animals', in D. Brothwell and E. Higgs (eds) 1970, *Science in archaeology. A survey of progress and research* New York, Praeger, 283–302

Spencer, B. 1983 'Limestone-tempered pottery from South Wales in the Late Iron Age and Early Roman Period', *Bull. Board Celtic Stud.* **30** pt. III, 405–19

Standing, I.J. 2000 'Ironworking Residues', in E. Price 2000, 92–4

Stace, C. 1997 *A New British Flora* Cambridge, Cambridge University Press

Stevens, C.J. 2009 'The Iron Age agricultural economy', in J. Wright, M. Leivers, R. Seager-Smith and C.J. Stevens 2009, *Cambourne New Settlement: Iron Age and Romano-British settlement on the clay uplands of west Cambridgeshire* WA Report **23**, Salisbury, Wessex Archaeology, 78–83

Stickler, T. 2003 'Animal bone', in A. Thomas, N. Holbrook and C. Bateman 2003, 57–61

Stuart-Macadam, P. 1991 'Anemia in Roman Britain. Poundbury Camp', in H. Bush and Z. Zvelebil (eds) 1991, *Health in past socieities: Biocultural interpretations of human skeletal remains in archaeological contexts* BAR Int. Ser. **659**, Oxford, Archaeopress, 101–13

Teichert, M. 1975 'Osteometrische Untersuchungen zur Berechnung der Widerristhöhe bei Schafen', in A.T. Clason (ed.) 1975, *Archaeozoological studies: Papers of the Archaeozoological conference 1974, held at the Biologisch-Archaeologisch Instituut of the State University of Groningen* Amsterdam, North Holland Publishing, 51–69

Thomas, A., Holbrook, N. and Bateman, C. 2003 *Later Prehistoric and Romano-British burial and settlement at Hucclecote, Gloucestershire* Bristol Gloucestershire Archaeol. Rep. **2**, Cirencester, Cotswold Archaeology

Timby, J. 1987 'Other Roman Pottery', in P. Ellis 1987, 77–92

Timby, J. 2000 'Pottery', in E. Price 2000, 125–62

Tomber, R. and Dore, J. 1998 *The National Roman Fabric Reference Collection: A Handbook* London, Museum of London Archaeology Service

Trotter, M. and Gleser, G.C. 1952 'Estimation of stature from long bones of American Whites and Negroes', *American J. Physical Anthropol.* **10** (4), 463–514

Trotter, M. and Gleser, G.C. 1958 'A re-evaluation of estimation of stature based on measurements of stature taken during life and of long bones after death', *American J. Physical Anthropol.* **16** (1), 79–123

van Arsdell, R.D. 1989 *Celtic Coinage of Britain* London, Spink and Son

van der Merwe, A.E., Steyn, M. and Maat, G.J.R. 2010 'Adult scurvy in skeletal remains of late 19th century mineworkers in Kimberey, South Africa', *Int. J. Osteoarchaeol.* **20** (3), 307–16

van der Veen, M. 1989 'Charred grain assemblages from Roman-Period corn driers in Britain', *Archaeol. J.* **146**, 302–19

von den Driesch, A. 1976 *A guide to the measurement of animal bones from archaeological sites* Peabody Museum Bulletins **1**, Cambridge, Harvard University

Vretemark, M. 1997 *Från ben till boskap: Kosthåll och djurhållning med utgångspunkt i medeltida benmaterial* från Skara Skrifter från Länsmuseet Skara **25**, Skara, Skaraborgs länsmuseum

WA (Wessex Archaeology) 2004 'New Moreton Farm, Standish, Gloucestershire: Interim Report on an Archaeological Evaluation', unpublished Wessex Archaeology report **55760**

Walker, G., Langton, B. and Oakey, N. 2001 *An Iron Age site at Groundwell West, Wiltshire: Excavations in 1996* Cirencester, Cotswold Archaeological Trust

Walker, P.L., Bathurst, R.R., Richman, R., Gjerdrum, T. and Andrushko, V.A. 2009 'The causes of porotic hyperostosis and cribra orbitalia: a reappraisal of the iron-deficiency-anemia hypothesis', *American J. Physical Anthropol.* **139** (2), 109–25

Watters, J. 2011 'BH-343C86: A Roman Bracelet', http://beta.finds.org.uk/database/artdatabase/artefacts/record/id/462749 (accessed: 19 Mar 2013).

Webster, P.V. 1976 'Severn Valley ware: A Preliminary Study', *Trans. Bristol Gloucestershire Archaeol. Soc.* **94**, 18–46

Wheeler, E.A., Baas, P. and Gasson, P.E. 1989 'IAWA list of microscopic features for hardwood identification', *IAWA Bulletin n.s.* **10** (3), 219–332

Young A. 2009a 'Fox's Field, Ebley Road, Stonehouse, Gloucestershire: Archaeological Evaluation Project', unpublished report for Avon Archaeological Unit

Young, C.J. 1977a *Oxfordshire Roman pottery* BAR Brit. Ser. **43**, Oxford, British Archaeological Reports

Young, T. 1977b 'Site Reports: Stroud', *Glevensis* **11**, 30

Young, T.P. 2009b 'Archaeometallurgical Residues', in M. Brett, E. McSloy, and N. Holbrook 2009, 'A Roman enclosure at Crickhowell Road, Trowbridge, Cardiff: Evaluation and Excavation 2005–06', *Archaeol. Cambrensis* **158**, 155–9

MEDIEVAL ENCLOSURES AND A FISHPOND AT RECTORY MEADOWS, KINGS STANLEY: EXCAVATIONS IN 2011

by Alan Hardy and Jamie Wright

with contributions by
Sarah Cobain, Angus Crawford and Jonny Geber

INTRODUCTION

Between June and July 2011, Cotswold Archaeology (CA) carried out an archaeological excavation in the grounds of The Rectory, Church Street, Kings Stanley (centred on NGR: SO 8105 0362; Fig. 1). The work was undertaken on behalf of Colburn Homes Ltd as a condition of Planning Consent for 15 dwellings. The excavation was undertaken in accordance with a brief prepared by Charles Parry, Senior Archaeological Officer, Gloucestershire County Council (archaeological advisors to the local planning authority, Stroud District Council), who also monitored both the fieldwork and the post-excavation analysis.

Site location, geology and topography

The site lies centrally to modern village and just over 50m to the west of Church Street, on ground sloping gently down to the west from 46m AOD. It is about 500m to the south of the church of St George's, and about 250m north of the area known as 'The Borough', which contained the medieval market place (Tilley *et al.* 2007, 20). Immediately to the east of the site lie a medieval rectory and its associated buildings, including a late 16th-century dovecote (Herbert 1972a, 254).

The church stands on an outcrop of river gravels, while the southern core area of settlement sits on a bed of Dyrham Silts (BGS 1975). Church Street, which links the two areas, lies on a band of Lower Lias clay. Small streams on either side of the village flow north to the River Frome, the western stream forming the parish boundary with Leonard Stanley (Tilley *et al.* 2007, 19).

Historical and archaeological background

The early focus of settlement at Kings Stanley seems to have been around the church at the north end of the village. Extensive excavations in the immediate vicinity of the church, manor, and associated earthworks from the 1960s to the 1980s revealed a sequence of prehistoric, Roman and medieval occupation, much of it high status in character (Heighway 1989). Although the Norman church was established here, later medieval settlement developed some distance to the south of this. A settlement '*Stantone*' was mentioned in Domesday, was 'Stanley' from 1160, and added the prefix 'Kings' by 1278. As by this time the manor was held by the King, this distinguished it from the settlement of Leonard Stanley, its western neighbour, whose manor was held by Gloucester Abbey (Tilley *et al.* 2007, 20). In 1253 the lord of the manor, Adam le Despenser, was granted a market and fair, which

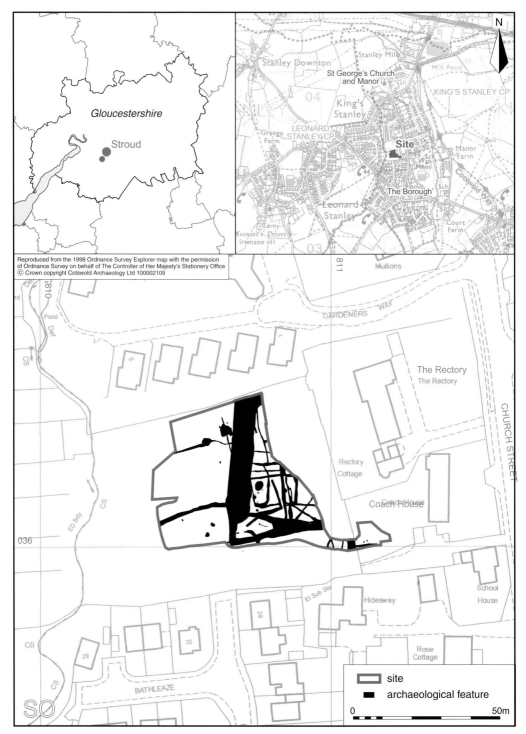

Fig. 1   Site location plan and all-feature plan (1:1250)

led to the establishment of a borough, sited some 750m south of the church and manor, and concentrated around the junction of the road leading northwards to the church with the east-west road skirting the heights of Selsey Common to the south. The new borough was not commercially successful, and by the 16th century was largely moribund. The post-medieval clothing industry prompted a revival in the settlement's fortunes, at least until the 19th century (Tilley *et al.*, 20).

No archaeological excavations have taken place in the area of the borough, or along the linking road (Church Street). Nevertheless, isolated finds of 13th-century pottery have been made in the area of The Beeches, on the western side of Church Street approximately mid-way between the present site and the church (Heighway 2007), and sherds of 'early medieval' pottery have also been found at a number of locations on both sides of Church Road (Peter Griffin, pers. comm.).

The eastern part of the site lies within property acquired by the rectory during the late 13th or 14th century. The western part, which prior to development comprised an acre of pasture bordering the parish boundary stream, is first recorded in 1588 as being granted by Elizabeth I to one Edward Wymark. By 1717 it had become incorporated with another parcel of land to the east as charity land (known as Deacon's Close), whose rental proceeds were administered by the church for the support of three local schools. Only in the 19th century did it become fully part of the rectory grounds (Charity Commission 1826–7). The earliest known detailed map of the area, the Kings Stanley Parish Map of 1817, shows the rectory and associated buildings occupying two plots fronting the road (Fig. 2). Deacon's

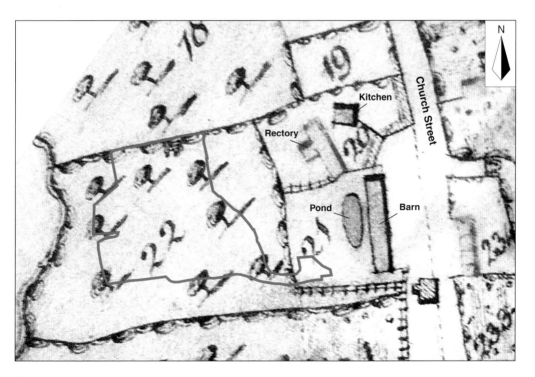

Fig. 2   Detail of the Rectory and Deacon's Close from the 1817 Parish Map (GRO: D1159)

Fig. 3   The central part of the site under excavation, with infilled pond 1375 visible as the darker area to the centre, looking north.

Close (no. 22 on the map) is still depicted as a separate plot, with independent access to the road.

Methodology

An area of 2000m² was mechanically stripped, and all revealed features were sample-excavated by hand (10% of linear features; 50-100% of discrete features). The exception was a large infilled pond that crossed the centre of the site from north to south (Fig. 3), which was recorded via two trenches machined through it (Fig. 4). All features were cut into the natural light greyish brown clay natural, and sealed by a subsoil and turf/topsoil layer typically 0.2m deep. Suitable deposits within features were sampled for macrofossil and/or charcoal remains. Two monolith samples were taken from the stratigraphic sequence through the pond. All recording followed standard CA procedures.

EXCAVATION RESULTS

A network of features was revealed in the centre of the site, representing a sequence of intercutting enclosures (Fig. 5) defined by shallow gullies. Their stratigraphic relationships

Fig. 4   One of two trenches excavated across infilled pond 1375, looking south-east.

were frequently inconclusive and their artefactual dating lacked precision as much of the dating material, by virtue of the repeated disturbance of earlier features, had been subject to redeposition. Thus a confident interpretation of the sequence of enclosures has not been possible, and neither has an accurate chronology. However, through consideration of spatial relationships and the general distribution of finds, a plausible sequence of four phases of enclosure can be postulated, dated to the 12th/13th centuries by the predominant pottery recovered from them. A quantity of residual Roman pottery was also recovered from features within these phases. This material is discussed below.

Slightly later pottery (Minety ware) and a different alignment indicated a change of land division in the later 13th century (Phase F), and this was followed by late medieval Phases G and H. The final phase (Phase J) is dated by pottery of 18th or 19th-century date.

Period 1: 12th century?

A shallow gully (1167, 1176), orientated north-east/south-west, was identified on the eastern edge of the main part of the site. Its orientation was distinctly different to other alignments, although its profile and fill characteristics were similar. Stratigraphically it appeared to be the earliest feature (Phase A) revealed in this area, although there was no artefactual evidence that it represented pre-medieval activity.

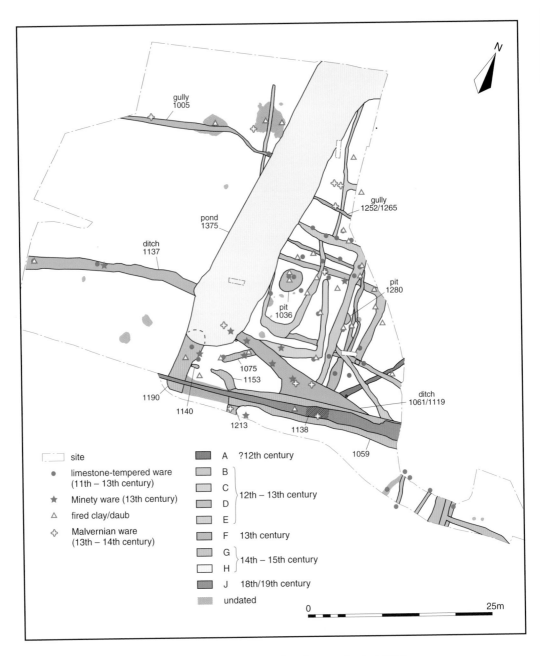

Fig. 5   Phase plan of the excavation, with pottery distributions (scale 1:500)

Period 2: 12th to early 13th century

This period was represented by four successive rectangular or subrectangular paddocks (enclosures B, C, D and E), defining small areas. Although enclosure C was on a slightly different alignment from the others, it was noticeable that all the enclosures tended to occupy the same confined area, and the western part of the site extending downslope towards the parish boundary stream remained clear. Most of the enclosure gullies were less than 0.2m deep and were a shallow 'U' shape in profile. By contrast, the ditches of the last enclosure in the sequence (E), displayed a steep 'V'-shaped profile averaging 0.6m deep. The gully fills were generally silty clay with occasional inclusions of fired-clay fragments. Finds from these features included 11th to 13th-century limestone-tempered pottery in generally small quantities. Animal bone was also recovered in small quantities, principally elements of mature cattle, but also of pig. The distribution pattern of this material was similar to that of the limestone-tempered pottery. Exceptionally, enclosure B yielded a substantial quantity of Roman pottery from a single section.

Two discrete features, large pit 1036 and small pit 1280, were located within the complex of gullies and both were presumably associated with one of the enclosures. The former was a substantial feature, approximately 3m in diameter but less than 0.4m deep. It contained a mixed silty clay fill, with fragments of fired clay and limestone rubble. A quantity of limestone-tempered 11th to 13th-century pottery was also recovered, along with some animal bone. Although two possible postholes and an undated shallow pit were identified close by, there was no evidence of a structural function for pit 1036, nor was there evidence that it was dug to hold water. The likelihood is that this pit was excavated to obtain material for wall daub, or clay for an oven. It did not appear to have been used as a rubbish pit, which suggests that any domestic focus was some distance away.

In the narrow south-eastern extension of the site, a number of linear features were identified (1048, 1055, 1057), which, by their profile and from the finds recovered, were likely to be parts of the same succession of enclosures. Their location and approximate orientation broadly coincided with a modern hedge line (Fig. 1) apparent as a boundary between plots 21 and 22 on the 1817 Parish map (Fig. 2).

Period 3: 13th century

A reorganisation of the site was indicated by two linear features: in the north, gullies 1005 and 1252/1265; and in the south, ditches 1137 and 1061/1119 (Phase F). In contrast to earlier activity, these features extended across the western part of the site, turning to a more east/west orientation towards the western limit of excavation. The fills of the southern ditch (1119) yielded a quantity of Minety Ware sherds, consistent with a date in the later 13th century.

Period 4: 14th to 15th century

A further reorganisation of the site was indicated by the northern boundary of an enclosure (1059) at the southern edge of the site, which turned to the south as ditch 1213 (Phase G). A north/south ditch (1190) was also revealed, terminating immediately south of pond 1375 (see below). These two features appeared to have been linked by small gullies 1140 and 1153, which may have defined a gateway.

To the north was a large shallow pond (1375), over 40m long and averaging 7.3m wide by 1.3m deep, with sloping sides and a flat base (Phase H). The rounded southern terminus of the pond was exposed, truncating the northern terminus of ditch 1190. The pond extended beyond the northern limit of excavation, though a curve in its eastern side suggested that it may have turned or widened at this point. The fills of the pond were mostly recorded in a machine-cut slot near its southern terminus (Fig. 4), which revealed two layers of primary silting of grey clay (1379, 1380), followed by a deposit of mottled greyish brown clay. Monolith samples of these deposits were taken and analysed (see *Plant macrofossils and charcoal*, below).

Period 5: 18th to 19th century

The final phase of activity was represented by an episode of consolidation in the southern part of the site (Phase J). Deposits of limestone rubble and gravel were dumped along the length of ditch 1059 and also as other patches in the vicinity. At a point where the line of ditch 1059 crossed that of earlier medieval enclosure ditches of enclosures D and E, the consolidation took a more substantial form. A stone-built channel (1138) was constructed within the upper fill of ditch 1059, measuring 2.84m long, its east end terminating in a faced stone edge (Fig. 6). The west end did not display any evidence of a similar finish, although it may have been disturbed by more recent activity. The structure appeared originally to have been capped with slabs, and a substantial quantity of stone rubble bordered each side of the channel, suggesting that the whole structure may have been a north/south crossing over an otherwise boggy drainage ditch, the stone structure providing a firm surface while still allowing water to pass underfoot through the channel.

Fig. 6   Stone channel 1138, looking west. Scales 1m and 0.3m.

THE FINDS AND ENVIRONMENTAL EVIDENCE

Pottery, by Angus Crawford

The assemblage of 461 sherds of pottery, weighing 9.3kg, dates predominantly to the medieval period, though a small number of Roman, post-medieval and modern sherds were also recovered (Table 1). The level of preservation varies, with the majority of the Roman sherds in poor condition, and a large number of the medieval of sherds having abraded edges and vesicular surfaces due to the leaching of calcareous inclusions. The assemblage was fully recorded, sorted by fabric and quantified utilizing sherd count, weight and rim Estimated Vessel Equivalents. For pottery identified as of a likely Worcestershire type, the fabric code used for Deansway, Worcestershire (Bryant 2004) has been adopted. Otherwise fabric codes have been created for the purpose of this report and, where possible, Roman fabrics have been correlated to the National Roman Fabric Reference Collection (Tomber and Dore 1998).

Table 1: Roman and medieval pottery by fabric (quantification, sherd count, weight in grams and rim EVEs)

Date	Fabric	Description/Reference	Ct.	Wt. (g)	Rim EVE
Roman	SVW OX2	Oxidised Severn Valley ware (Tomber and Dore 1998, 149)	8	54	-
		Oxidised organically-tempered Severn Valley Ware	8	33	-
		Reduced organically-tempered Severn Valley ware	2	16	-
	DOR BB1	Dorset Black-burnished ware 1 (Tomber and Dore 1998, 127)	5	41	.09
	LEZ SA2	Central Gaulish samian ware (Tomber and Dore 1998, 30)	2	21	-
	GWs	Sandy Greywares	10	43	.03
	GWco	Coarse Greyware with organic inclusions	1	4	-
	REDg	Reduced fabric with grog inclusions	1	22	.07
	Oxf	Fine oxidised fabric	5	8	.07
	Oxs	Sandy oxidised fabric	5	49	-
	Oxorg	Sandy oxidised fabric with organic inclusions	1	10	-
		Total	*48*	*301*	
Medieval	Oolitic_LT	Oolitic limestone–tempered ware (Ireland 1998)	279	6181	1.99
	MIN_LT	Minety ware (Musty 1973)	60	1816	1.07
	MALV	Unglazed Malvernian ware (Bryant 2004)	25	292	.13
	OXS	Sandy oxidised ware	14	94	-
	OXSgorg	Sandy oxidised ware with grog and organic inclusions	1	7	-
	OXSorg	Sandy oxidised ware with organic inclusions	1	6	-
	REDS	Reduced (brown) sandy ware	5	51	-
	WORCS	Worcester-type sandy unglazed ware (Bryant 2004)	2	37	.10
	WORCSG	Worcester-type sandy glazed ware (Bryant 2004)	1	13	-
	Bsgo	Black sandy ware with grog and organic inclusions	1	11	-
	LTS	Limestone-tempered ware	1	6	-
		Total	*390*	*8514*	

Roman pottery

A small Roman pottery assemblage totalling 48 sherds and weighing 301g was recovered from six stratified deposits and from the topsoil. All sherds are abraded with only four deposits containing solely Roman material, from Phase A (fill 1177 of gully 1176), enclosure B (fill 1181 of gully 1180; fill 1354 of gully 1355) and Phase J (fill 1179 of gully 1178).

The Roman pottery assemblage is dominated by Severn Valley wares (Tomber and Dore 1998; type SVW OX2) with 18 sherds, weighing 103g. Of these, eight are of oxidised type with a further eight organically-tempered variants and two with a reduced, organically-tempered fabric. While the Seven Valley wares can only be broadly dated to the Roman period, a 1st to 2nd-century AD date for the organically-tempered variants is likely. Greywares are the next most common fabric type, with ten sherds (43g) in a fine sandy fabric with a coarse sandy sherd with organic inclusions also present. All of the greywares are probably of local production and, as the sherds are unfeatured, are attributed a broad Roman period date.

A small quantity (5 sherds weighing 41g) of Dorset Black-burnished ware sherds (Tomber and Dore 1998; type DOR BB1) are present, again attributed to a broad date of 2nd to 4th century AD. A sherd from fill 1181 of ditch 1182 (enclosure B), featuring a wide flaring everted rim, is consistent with jars produced during the 3rd and 4th centuries AD. The remaining Roman assemblage includes two sherds of central Gaulish samian (Tomber and Dore 1998; type LEZ SA2), in poor condition, from fill 1068 of the pond, 1375. Unfeatured sherds in fine and sandy oxidised fabrics, some with organic inclusions and a reduced grogged fabric, are also present. Although residual, a 2nd-century AD date can be applied to the samian, with the remainder assignable only to the broader Roman period.

Medieval pottery

The medieval pottery assemblage amounts to 390 sherds (8.5kg) and is characterised by an abundance of limestone-tempered wares (87% of the total medieval pottery count). The majority of the medieval pottery consists of cooking pot-type coarse wares.

Vesicular fabric Oolitic_LT amounts to 279 sherds and almost certainly represents a leached limestone-tempered type very common from the Cotswold region (Ireland 1998). A further sherd retaining oolitic limestone inclusions, though in a sandier fabric, is considered to be in the same Cotswold oolitic limestone-fabric tradition. Identifiable vessel forms are restricted to jar/cooking pots with everted rims. Rim morphology varies, with examples from simple everted rims of uniform thickness to those with thickened/expanded outer proportions. Two sherds with everted inturned rims were also recorded from fill 1212 (ditch 1213, enclosure G) and fill 1276 (gully 1275, enclosure D) (Fig. 7, no. 1). A jar with a clubbed rim of 11th to 12th-century date was recorded from fill 1286 of pit 1284 (enclosure B), but the small size of the group makes determining whether there is any chronological significance to rim variation problematic.

Sherds in a well-fired oolitic limestone-tempered fabric (MIN_LT) with a sparse lead glaze are identifiable as Minety-type ware. Dating for the unfeatured sherds is broad with production of Minety wares extending between the 12th and 15th centuries. Identifiable vessel forms include jars with everted rims, of uniform or thickened types, of 14th to 15th-century date. A double-handled spouted pitcher, of handmade type, features applied strips and combing to the body as well as stab decoration to the handles (Fig. 7, no. 2). Recovered

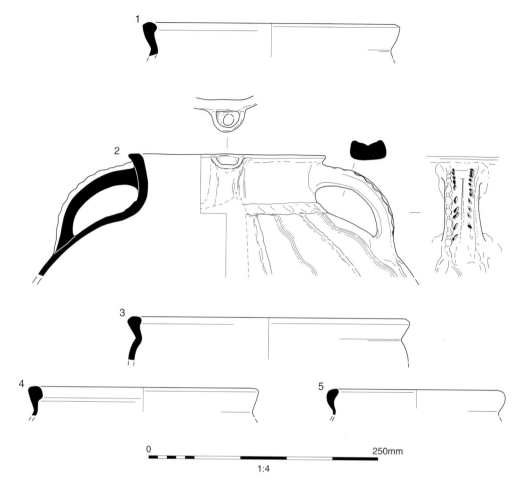

Fig. 7   Medieval pottery (1:4)

as joining sherds from ditch fill deposits 1189 and 1191 (both from ditch 1190, enclosure G); a late 12th or early 13th-century date can be attributed to the vessel. A rim from a globular jar, recovered from the upper fill 1342 of ditch 1341 (enclosure F), probably of 14th or 15th-century date, confirms a broad period of use for Minety wares on site.

Other regional wares include 21 sherds of unglazed Malvernian ware (MALV), with a possible further four sherds also included. All are typified by inclusions of moderate to abundant Malvernian rock (acid igneous) inclusions. Where present, rim forms are of short everted and folded type (Fig. 7, no. 3) typical of cooking pots produced during the 13th and 14th centuries (Bryant 2004, 298–9).

Three sherds with abundant medium rounded sub-angular quartz inclusions are identifiable as likely Worcestershire types (fabrics WORSC and WORCSG; Bryant 2004). Two sherds are unglazed and include a jar with an everted and thickened rim, which probably dates from the 13th to mid-14th century (Fig. 7, no. 4). The remaining sherd is oxidised with an internal glaze, possibly from a bowl or skillet of 14th-century type (ibid., 290–7). Further oxidised sherds include 14 in a sandy fabric (OXS), with one also featuring organic inclusions (OXSorg) and another with grog and organic inclusions (OXSgorg). None of the sherds could be identified to source though a local production is possible. The remaining medieval pottery consists of small individual sherds that cannot be identified further beyond attributing a broad medieval date of production.

Post-medieval and modern

The small post-medieval and modern pottery assemblage (49 sherds) comprises a range of domestics wares utilized during the 18th to 20th century. A range of plain glazed earthenwares, including North Devon gravel-tempered ware, are datable across the 17th to 18th centuries. Refined whitewares fabrics, which includes pearlwares, blue-on-white transfer printed wares and a piece from a transfer-printed porcelain sanitary ware bowl are considered to date after 1780.

Discussion

The Roman pottery assemblage is of limited interpretative value. The small quantities and poor condition suggest some degree of residuality within the assemblage. This material may have derived from deposition on the ground surface prior to being incorporated into the ditch fills.

The medieval pottery consists of a limited range of pottery types. The forms are predominantly utilitarian jars and there is a high reliance on wares produced in the Cotswold oolitic limestone-tempered tradition. Whether this is through a deliberate preference or restricted access to a wider variety of products is difficult to interpret. That other material was available is evidenced by the Minety, Malvernian and Worcester-type products within the assemblage. With the exception of the Minety ware spouted pitcher, these wares again appear to be predominantly utilitarian in nature and the assemblage is consistent with a site of lower socio-economic status in the medieval period.

Other finds, by Angus Crawford

Fired clay/daub

A total of 322 pieces of fired clay and daub was recorded, weighing 6.21kg, of which 180 pieces were identified as daub with another 59 pieces recorded as daub-like material, recovered from medieval-dated deposits spanning the 11th, 12th and 13th centuries. The majority of this material featured stake or lath impressions, suggesting an association with structures, and possibly ovens. In addition two small fragments of fired clay, both from medieval contexts, appeared to have originated from objects and may have been mould or loomweight fragments.

Ceramic building material

Thirty-five fragments of ceramic building material, weighing 1.59kg, were recorded from the site. Most were undiagnostic and of medieval to modern in date; however, a fragment of Roman tile (340g), with a complete stamp of 'ARVERI', was recorded from deposit 1357 (pit 1036, Phase D) (see Fig. 8, no. 1). Another small fragment of Roman tile (6g) appeared to also have a small portion of an 'ARVERI' stamp, and was recovered from deposit 1332 (ditch 1331, enclosure E) (see Fig. 8, no. 2). The 'ARVERI' stamp is believed to be

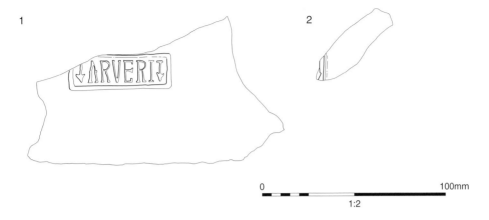

Fig. 8   Roman tile featuring the maker's stamp ARVERI (1:2)

from a private tile-maker working near Cirencester, though other places of manufacture are possible (see Collingwood and Wright 1993). A further likely fragment of Roman tile was recovered as an unstratified find.

Flint
Seven pieces of flint were recovered from the assemblage. Of these, a large core (1.26kg) in a honey-coloured flint was recovered as an unstratified find. The core is of interest as flint is not part of the local geology and the core would have to have been transported to the site. Further finds include a primary flake from an unphased tree-throw pit (1014), further flaked material from a natural hollow (1024), and others recovered as unstratified finds.

Glass
A small fragment of Roman blue-coloured glass (2g) was recorded from layer 1166, a spread of silty clay over part of ditch 1164 (Phase F).

Slag
Three pieces of tap slag were recorded, including two from gully 1034 (enclosure D) and ditch 1182 (enclosure B) on the east side of the site. The presence of this material suggests that some ironworking, possibly including smelting, was taking place nearby, although not to any intensive degree. A small assemblage of metal objects and clay-pipe fragments was also recovered. A full catalogue of all recovered finds is retained in the archive.

Animal bone, by Jonny Geber

Within the bone assemblage species were identified, but no quantitative analysis was viable for such a small assemblage. Only animal bones from medieval deposits were recorded in detail, and these are discussed as a collection broadly dating from the 11th to 13th century AD. Only a relatively small amount of animal bone was recovered (3kg), which nevertheless gives insights into the husbandry regime and economy of the site, and the diet of the people who occupied it. The bones were generally well preserved, but had in several cases suffered considerable fragmentation. The bones were identified to species and skeletal element with the aid of the Cotswold Archaeology osteological reference collection and reference literature (Iregren 2002; Radu 2005; Schmid 1972). Measurements were taken in accordance with von den Driesch (1976), and shoulder heights of cattle and horse were calculated using the equations by Fock (1966) and May (1985).

The main domesticates: cattle, caprovine and pig

Bones from mammals dominated the assemblage (Table 2). Of these, cattle amounted to 65% of all identified species by fragment count. These derived from a minimum of two mature and one juvenile animal. One metatarsal (GL = 210mm), sexed as cow (Chaplin 1971, 103–4), generated an estimated shoulder height of 112cm. One middle foot phalanx displayed considerable marginal osteophytosis at the proximal articulation, which indicates degenerative joint disease (Rogers and Waldron 1995).

The identified elements included both meat-rich and meat-poor elements, which would suggest that the animals slaughtered locally were also consumed in the vicinity. One noteworthy deposit (fill 1369 of pond 1375) included fragments of two bull skulls, a juvenile mandible, a third foot phalanx, a patella, and a fragment of a thoracic vertebra. With the exception of the patella and vertebra, all of these represent meat-poor regions of the carcass. This may suggest slaughter waste rather than generic domestic waste.

Eleven fragments derived from caprovines, which was the second most abundant species in the assemblage, although it was not possible to distinguish between sheep and goat from the remains. The material included two skull fragments and two loose teeth, a thoracic vertebra, two metapodials and four fragments of a minimum of three tibiae. One of the

Table 2:   Identified animal species from medieval deposits by fragment count (NISP), minimum number of individuals (MNI) and weight

Species	NISP	MNI	Weight (g)
MAMMALS			
Cattle *(Bos taurus)*	41	3	2,462.43
Caprovine *(Ovis aries/Capra hircus)*	11	2	106.16
Pig *(Sus scrofa domesticus)*	5	1	56.09
Horse *(Equus caballus)*	3	1	383.65
Dog *(Canis familiaris)*	3	1	51.87
Large sized	11	-	62.80
Medium sized	8	-	5.42
Indeterminable *(Mammalia sp.)*	122	-	17.96
Subtotal:	*204*	*8*	*3,146.38*
BIRDS			
Fowl *(Gallus gallus)*	1	1	0.80
Subtotal:	*1*	*1*	*0.80*
FISH			
Bream *(Abramis brama)*	6	1	0.05
Indeterminable *(Pisces sp.)*	4	-	0.03
Subtotal:	*10*	*1*	*0.08*
Totals:	*215*	*9*	*3.147.26*

tibiae, which comprised part of the leg meat-cut, displayed knife-cut marks from butchery on its posterior surface.

Five deposits each yielded a single pig bone fragment, which were identified as parts of a mandible, a loose tooth, a scapula, a humerus and a metapodial. The mandible derived from an immature animal, aged approximately 6–9 months (Habermehl 1975; Silver 1970). The generic zooarchaeological evidence from across medieval England has indicated a higher proportion of pig bones and a lesser proportion of caprovine on high-status sites compared with urban sites or villages (Grant 1988). The evidence from this assemblage suggests a low status for the medieval site.

Horse and dog
Three horse bones were present in the assemblage: two fragments of a skull from ditch 1119 (Phase F) and a metacarpal pit 1036 (Phase D). The skull included several molar teeth, which all displayed considerable wear which suggests an old age for this animal. A shoulder height of 135cm (13.1 hands) could be estimated from the metacarpals, which is of normal size for horses in Britain during the medieval period (Clark 2004, 22).

Dog was represented by one thoracic vertebra from ditch 1032 (enclosure D), and the left and right side of the same mandible in from ditch 1094 (enclosure C). The latter bones were fragmented, but suggest that they derived from an adult dog of medium size.

Bird
The only bird bone in the assemblage was a fowl tibio-tarsus found in gully 1275 (enclosure D). Evidently, fowl and egg would have contributed to the diet, although to what extent is not possible to determine. Bones from domestic birds are generally less common on lower status sites than higher status sites in the medieval period (Grant 1988). They are also, however, amongst the most fragile animal bones in archaeological assemblages, and this bias may be reflected in the relative quantities of recovered bone material.

Fish
Fish was represented by two scales and eight vertebrae found in three fills of pond 1375 (Phase H). Six of these could be identified as bream. The archaeological evidence of a fishpond on the site suggests that there would have been regular consumption of fish, and that the fish bones are from bream bred this pond. Bream is particularly well suited to ponds, as its preferred habitat is the bottom of stagnant and muddy water (Weiss Adamson 2004, 42). The consumption pattern of fish in the medieval period in Britain varied significantly depending on social status, resource availability, and religious standing (Serjeantson and Woolgar 2006). Based on the historical accounts and current archaeological evidence from elsewhere in Britain, the evidential access of pond fish at Kings Stanley during the late medieval period does imply a high social status consumption pattern (Dyer 1988; Woolgar 1999).

Plant macrofossils and charcoal, by Sarah Cobain

Introduction
Five bulk soil samples were taken for plant macrofossil and charcoal remains from medieval features pit 1036 (Phase D) and pond 1375 (Phase H). Following assessment, four of these samples were selected for detailed plant macrofossil and charcoal analysis to provide

Table 3: Plant macrofossil identifications

* = waterlogged; + = 1-4 items; ++ = 6-20 items; +++ = 21-40 items; ++++ = >40 items. Habitat preferences: A = arable weed; D = weed indicative of disturbed areas; P = grassland/pasture weed; M = marsh/wetland species; HSW = hedgerow/scrub/woodland species; E = economic species

Context number				1360	1357	1105	1379	1380
Feature number				**1036**	**1036**	**1375**	**1375**	**1375**
Sample number				53	54	55	60	61
Flot volume (ml)				2.5	11.5	290	410	195
Sample volume (l)				10	10	10	10	10
Soil remaining (l)				30	30	30	30	30
Phase				**D**	**D**	**H**	**H**	**H**
Plant macrofossil preservation				Poor	Poor	Good	Good	Good
Habitat Code	**Family**	**Species**	**Common Name**					
HSW	Adoxaceae	Sambucus nigra L.	Elder*	-	-	7	7	+
M	Apiaceae	Apium nodiflorum (L.) Lag.	Fool's-watercress	-	-	2	-	-
M		Apium repens (Jacq.) Lag./Apium graveolens L.	Creeping marshwort/wild celery*	-	-	16	2	-
M/D		Conium maculatum L.	Hemlock*	-	-	-	3	-
D/P	Asteraceae	Cirsium Mill./Carduus L.	Thistles*	-	-	31	21	-
HSW	Betulaceae	Corylus avellana L.	Hazelnut*	-	-	65	2	-
HSW		Corylus avellana L.	Whole hazelnuts*	-	-	9	-	-
M	Ceratophyllaceae	Ceratophyllum demersum L.	Rigid hornwort*	-	-	-	3	+
M/D	Cyperaceae	Carex L.	Sedges*	-	-	14	5	-
D/A/P	Fabaceae	Vicia L./Lathyrus L.	Vetches/vetchlings	-	9	1	5	-
D	Malvaceae	Malva L.	Mallows*	-	-	1	1	-
E	Poaceae	Avena L.	Oats grain	-	-	1	-	-
E		Hordeum vulgare	Hulled barley grain	1	3	-	2	-
E		Triticum aestivum L./Triticum Turgidum L./Triticum durum Desf.	Free-threshing wheat grain	5	28	2	10	+
E		Poaceae	Indeterminate cereal grain	10	21	8	6	++
D/A/P/M/HSW	Polygonaceae	Rumex L.	Docks	-	-	37	21	-
D/A/P/M/HSW		Rumex L.	Docks*	-	2	-	-	-
M	Potamogetonaceae	Potamogeton L.	Pondweeds*	-	-	-	10	-
M		Potamogeton cf crispus L.	cf curled pondweed*	-	-	-	61	-
P/D/A	Ranunculaceae	Ranunculus L.	Buttercups*	-	-	62	15	-
HSW	Rosaceae	Crataegus monogyna Jacq.	Hawthorn	-	-	-	1	-
HSW/D		Rubus L.	Bramble spp*	-	-	29	504	++
HSW/D		Rubus L.	Bramble thorns*	-	-	9	>500	+
HSW/D		Rubus L.	Bramble twigs with thorns*	-	-	-	11	-
HSW/D		Rubus sect. 2 Glandulosus Wimm. & Grab. (Rubus fruticosus L. agg.)	Bramble (blackberry)*	-	-	-	33	-
A/D		Solanum L.	Nightshades*	-	-	2	2	-
Total				16	64	295 (plus >500 bramble thorns)	720	2

information on the function of features sampled and socio-economic activities, and to infer the composition of the local woodlands and flora.

Methodology

Plant macrofossil and charcoal remains were retrieved by standard wet sieving and flotation procedures using a 250 micron sieve to collect the sieved/floated material. The seeds were identified using a low power stereo-microscope (Brunel MX1) (x10–x40). Identifications were carried out with reference to images and descriptions by Cappers *et al.* (2006), Berggren (1981) and Anderberg (1994). Up to 100 charcoal fragments of the >2mm sieve fraction were identified using an epi-illuminating microscope (Brunel SP400) (x40–x400). Identifications were carried out with reference to images and descriptions by Cutler and Gale (2000), Heller *et al.* (2004) and Wheeler *et al.* (1989). Nomenclature follows Stace (1997). The results are presented in Tables 3 and 4.

Results

Pit 1036

The basal and secondary fills within pit 1036 contained a small assemblage of carbonised cereal grains. Approximately half were identified as free-threshing wheat although they were highly abraded. There was no cereal chaff present. Free-threshing wheat was a typical crop during this period (Stone 2006, 13) and may have been exposed to heat, possibly while being dried in preparation for milling before being discarded in this pit.

A large amount of beech charcoal was also recovered from the pit. Approximately 40%

Table 4: Charcoal and waterlogged wood identifications
 * = waterlogged; + = 1-4 items; ++ = 6-20 items; +++ = 21-40 items; ++++ = >40 items;
 (s) = charcoal fragments typically too small to identify

Context number			1360	1357	1105	1379	1380
Feature number			**1036**	**1036**	**1375**	**1375**	**1375**
Sample number			53	54	55	60	61
Flot volume (ml)			2.5	11.5	290	410	195
Sample volume (l)			10	10	10	10	10
Soil remaining (l)			30	30	30	30	30
Phase			**D**	**D**	**H**	**H**	**H**
Charcoal quantity			++++ (s)	++++	++++	++ (s)	++ (s)
Charcoal preservation			Good	Good	N/A	Good	N/A
Family	**Species**	**Common Name**					
Betulaceae	*Alnus glutinosa (L.) Gaertn. /Corylus avellana L.*	Alder/hazel	-	1	-	-	-
	Betula L.	Birch	-	-	-	-	-
Fagaceae	*Fagus* L.	Beech	66	98	-	6	-
	Quercus robur L./*Quercus petraea* (Matt.) Liebl.	Pedunculate/sessile oak	-	1	-	-	-
Rosaceae	*Rubus* L.	Bramble twigs with thorns *	-	-	-	9	-
		Totals:	**66**	**100**	**0**	**15**	**0**

of the charcoal identified exhibited curved growth rings indicating that a proportion of the wood comprised small roundwood twigs. The remaining fragments may have originated from larger branches or trunk wood, although many were too small to be diagnostic. As there was no evidence of *in situ* burning, the material is likely to represent discarded firing debris from cereal-processing activities. The high proportion of roundwood may indicate coppicing of beech, although a larger number of charcoal samples would be required to confirm this.

Fishpond 1375

The two sections excavated through the medieval fishpond revealed a large number of well-preserved waterlogged and a small number of poorly-preserved carbonised seeds from fill 1105 (northern section) and fills 1379/1380 (southern section). The carbonised cereals consisted of abraded and most likely residual free-threshing wheat, barley and oat, typical of cereals cultivated during this period (Stone 2006, 13). The waterlogged plant macrofossils consisted of species indicative of wetland/marshland (rigid hornwort, pondweed, fool's-watercress), grassland (thistle spp and buttercup) and hedgerow/scrub/woodland (hazel, elder and brambles) environments (Stace 1997). The plant macrofossils were largely the same in both sections with the exception of fill 1105 (northern section) which contained a large number of waterlogged hazelnut-shell fragments and nine whole hazelnuts. In contrast, fill 1380 (southern section) contained large numbers of bramble thorns, blackberry and bramble spp. seeds. While as a whole this indicates the presence of a scrub landscape surrounding the pond, it also gives a very localised impression of vegetation with hazel tree(s) at the north end of the pond and brambles towards the south. Of the nine whole hazelnuts recovered, four of these had a small hole, <2mm diameter, at the top end of the nut, indicative of a nut weevil larvae (*Curculio nucum*) burrowing out of the nut. The female nut weevil lays its eggs which hatch inside the hazelnut and the larvae remain until they have eaten the entire nut, at which point they bore a hole out of the hazelnut.

Monoliths from fishpond 1375

Four monoliths of 500mm length were taken from one sequence of the fills of pond 1375, to examine the micromorphology of the pond fills. The surface of each monolith was cleaned using a scalpel to ensure the exposed layer of sediment was clean and remove smearing.

The layers identified within the monolith concur with those recorded on site (see *Excavation Results*, above) with the exception of a dark grey organic-rich layer 0.02m deep at the interface of pond fills 1379 and 1380, which represent the formation of 'gyttja': an anaerobic fine-grained, organic silt which develops in ponds, lakes or slow-moving water, building up in the base of the pond. The dark grey layer recorded between fills 1379 and 1380 may represent the growth of water plants the base of the pond during an interval when the pond base was dry. Eventually the pond was infilled with a grey-brown silty clay material (deposits 1378, 1377 and 1376). The water table in the area varied over time as some of this infilling material appears gleyed. This showed most clearly as bands within deposit 1378, and most likely represents a fluctuating winter/summer water table in the years after infilling.

Conclusions

The material recovered from this site provides an interesting reconstruction of the local vegetation together with an indication of crops being processed in this area during the medieval period. Fishpond 1375 contained a large, well preserved assemblage of waterlogged plant remains consisting of species indicative of wetland, grassland and hedgerow/scrub/woodland environments. Of particular interest was the dominance of hazelnut in the northern section of the pond and brambles in the southern section giving a localised impression of the vegetation. The pit and fishpond contained small assemblages of carbonised cereals dominated by free-threshing wheat, which were poorly preserved and highly abraded, and indicate discarded burnt waste from cereal-processing activities.

DISCUSSION

The Roman evidence (2nd to 3rd century AD)

While the occasional sherd of Roman pottery on the site might be accounted for by manuring, the presence of 19 sherds from at least three vessels in one ditch section (1182, enclosure B) on the eastern side of the site is significant. The stratigraphy of the ditch gave no indication that it did not belong with the rest of the 11th to 13th-century enclosure complex, and it is probable that this Roman pottery was redeposited when the ditch was infilled during one of the episodes of reorganisation of the enclosures. However, the presence of this quantity of Roman pottery suggests a 2nd to 3rd-century AD domestic focus nearby, distinct from the Roman site in the vicinity of the church, 500m to the north (Heighway 1989, 42). This contention is given support by the presence of fragments of two 'ARVERI'- stamped roof tiles (Fig. 8), suggesting that at least one Roman building of some status once stood nearby. The manorial and church focus to the north had its predecessor in a villa on the site (ibid., 42); the evidence from the current site invites the suggestion that the southern focus of settlement at Kings Stanley may also have had a Roman antecedent.

The medieval enclosures (12th to 13th centuries)

Some slight evidence of post-Roman occupation was recovered from the church and manor excavations (Heighway 1989, 37–8), but no similar indications were found on the current site (or have been found in the vicinity). The earliest identifiable activity on the site was the sequence of shallow gullies defining small paddocks (enclosures B, C, D and E) probably relating to plots fronting the southern part of Church Street, and bordering a meadow alongside the parish boundary stream. The gullies appeared to have acted as drainage channels, defining and draining small paddocks for livestock. They may well have been augmented with hurdles or light fences, which would not have left an archaeological footprint.

The pottery and the animal bone evidence are consistent with low-status occupation in the 12th to 13th centuries, during the period of the small enclosures. The dating suggests this activity took place before the formal establishment of the borough in the mid-13th century. Large sherds of a 12th to 13th-century spouted Minety Ware pitcher were recovered from the boundary ditch that was later expanded to become the pond, although the rest of the Minety ware, generally confined to the southern part of the site, is slightly later in date, indicating continued activity well into the 14th century, and even the 15th century. The environmental evidence from the large pit 1036 suggests the proximity of domestic activity, including crop-processing activity and the use of beech twigs, possibly as fuel.

Artefact distribution

Although redistribution of material was inevitable during the succession of enclosures, the process would not have moved the material far; thus a distribution plot of the earlier pottery and the fired clay suggests a concentration of earlier activity in and around the four enclosures B, C, D, and E. Although no footprint of a structure was identified, the fired clay, much of it displaying wattle impressions, suggests the presence of a building or possibly an oven in the vicinity.

The fishpond (14th to 15th centuries)

The character of the site changed significantly in the later medieval period with the construction of the large linear pond across much of the site (Phase H). The apparent return of the feature to the east, at the northern edge of the site, invites the suggestion that it could have acted as a moat, as well as a pond. In parts of lowland England, particularly the east Midlands, East Anglia and the South East, partially or fully encompassing moats were highly desirable as both defensive features and as status symbols in the 12th and 13th centuries (Steane 1985, 59), although there is much less evidence for their attraction in the South West. In the later medieval period the incidence of partial moats increased, a reflection of the desire for the status symbol without necessarily the physical constriction that a full moat would provide (ibid., 59). In contrast to the environmental evidence from the earlier paddocks and gullies, that from the pond/moat fill supports the hypothesis of a garden feature, with no evidence for domestic activity nearby. Hazel trees bordered it to the north, and brambles to the south, although this may be more indicative of the pond's dereliction, rather than the surrounding environment when it was in use.

As Bowden reminds us, not every medieval linear water-filled feature was a moat, and not every pond was intended to accommodate fish (2006, 173). However, such water features did also serve that purpose (Clarke 1984, 56–7), and the presence of scales and vertebrae from the pond clearly indicates it contained bream that was destined, one assumes, for the rectory dining table, even if it was also a decorative garden feature. This role was probably a reflection of the ecclesiastical associations of the property. The disparity of archaeological remains revealed on either side of the pond suggests that its creators made use of an existing boundary ditch, enlarging it to create the pond. This is supported by the evidence of the truncated earlier ditch (1190; Phase G) at the southern terminus of the pond.

The pond only produced late medieval dating evidence, so seems to have been a rather transient landscape feature. It is not shown on the earliest known map of the area, dating to 1817 (see Fig. 2), nor is it mentioned in the earliest terriers relating to the property, dating from 1618 (GDR: Glebe Terrier). Its infilling may relate to the alterations to the property undertaken by the rector Thomas Morgan in 1720; the terriers suggest that the preoccupation at the time was over the symmetry in garden planning (Peter Griffin, pers. comm.). The pond's alignment would have been at odds with that of the rectory building, and this may have led to its removal as a landscape feature. The 1817 Parish map shows no evidence of any remnant earthwork where the modern excavation found the pond, although it does show an oval pond immediately west of the long rectangular building to the south of the rectory. This building is presumably the barn and stable of '9 bays' recorded in the 1807 survey (GDR: Kings Stanley Terrier). That pond was infilled before the end of the 19th century, and the long barn was shortened and converted to a Coach House.

Landscape morphology

The phenomenon of polyfocal settlements was first examined in the standard work by Taylor (1977), and more recently by Aston (1985, 73–6). The incidence of polyfocal settlements in medieval England is more common than used to be thought, as often progressive infilling has tended to blend original multiple foci into one sprawling settlement. As for Kings Stanley, its medieval polyfocalism is more marked than most, with an apparent gap of some 750m between the medieval manor and church, and the established borough. The evidence from Rectory Meadows allows some informed if tentative conclusions to be drawn.

The alignment of features, both in the existing landscape and as revealed in the archaeo-logical excavation, show an interesting divergence over time. The early sequence of en-closures (B–E) appears to broadly respect the alignments of the properties to the south of the site, suggesting that this area may have originally been part of the mid-13th century market establishment, or even part of a putative predecessor. It is possibly significant that the present Coach House (of probable medieval origin) is also aligned in respect of this earlier arrangement. The later, larger plot boundaries (Phase F) across the site appear to have respected the property alignments to the north along the west side of Church Street, as does the rectory building itself. It is also significant that the medieval plot boundaries F extended right across the site towards the stream, suggesting that for a time they denoted divisions of the pasture later known as Deacon's Close. The later fishpond reverted to the earlier alignment, although this seems to have been so because it was created from an earlier phase of boundary ditch.

The dating evidence would suggest, therefore, that the establishment of a market in the middle of the 13th century was not a brand new settlement, but possibly involved the con-solidation and expansion of an existing hamlet or node of settlement at the junction of a track running south from the manor and church, and a west-east route linking Frocester, Leonard Stanley and Woodchester, running under the scarp of Selsey Common to the south.

The site later occupied by the rectory appears to have been originally laid out in respect of the prevailing boundaries of plots to the south, and may have represented the most northerly of the properties of the southern focus of settlement. The dating evidence suggests that this could well have dated to the 12th century, or even earlier.

In contrast, the orientation of the boundaries of the rectory building echo those of the properties to the north, and those on the eastern side of Church Street. It is possible therefore, that the rectory property represents a subsequent infilling of the space between the burgeoning market settlement to the south and the focal point of the manor and the church to the north.

The regional context

Gloucestershire saw significant prosperity in the 12th and 13th centuries, based largely on the burgeoning wool trade, but also on manufactured cloth (Tilley et al. 2007, 21). The location of the rectory, a considerable distance from the church and on the northern edge of the newly founded borough, may reflect the desire of the Church to maintain some sort of ecclesiastical presence close to the new settlement.

The evidence of post-Conquest development of the settlement of Kings Stanley corres-ponds to the regional pattern. Its neighboring settlement Leonard Stanley also prospered into the 13th century, in this case with the benefaction of a priory set up by Gloucester Abbey. It too benefited from a weekly market set up in the 13th century. The boom in the cloth industry of the 13th and 14th centuries in the region appears not have directly benefited the market of Kings Stanley; its neighbour's commercial fortunes seem to have been managed with much greater success, such that by 1650, Leonard Stanley was described as a 'market town' in a survey of church livings, while Kings Stanley was not (Herbert 1972, 253).

Conclusions

The northern part of Kings Stanley has benefited from extensive archaeological investigation in recent decades. The southern focus has yet to receive such attention, yet the excavations at Rectory Meadows suggest that there could well be an equally complex narrative to be understood there.

ACKNOWLEDGEMENTS

The entire project was funded by Colburn Homes, to whom, in the person of Martin Evans, must go appreciation for their support and cooperation. The excavation was supervised by Jamie Wright, and the post-excavation programme was managed by Joern Schuster and Alan Hardy. Illustrations are by Lorna Gray. Alan Hardy would like to express his thanks to Peter Griffin and Carolyn Heighway for freely giving of their time and knowledge of the history and archaeology of Kings Stanley. The project archive is currently held by Cotswold Archaeology. It will be duly deposited with The Museum in the Park, Stroud, Gloucestershire, under the accession number STGCM 2011.33.

BIBLIOGRAPHY

Primary Sources

GRO (Gloucestershire Archives):
  GRO/D1159 1817 Parish Map of Kings Stanley, Gloucestershire

GDR (Gloucester Diocesan Records):
  1618 Glebe Terrier
  1807 Kings Stanley Terrier

Secondary Sources

Anderberg, A-L. 1994 *Atlas of seeds: Part 4* Uddevalla, Swedish Museum of Natural History
Aston, M. 1985 *Interpreting the Landscape: Landscape Archaeology and Local History* London, Batsford
Berggren, G. 1981 *Atlas of seeds: Part 3* Arlöv, Swedish Museum of Natural History
BGS (British Geological Survey) 1975 *1:50,000 Geological Survey of Great Britain (England and Wales), Solid and Drift, map sheet 234: Gloucester* Keyworth, British Geological Survey
Bowden, M. 2006 'The Medieval Countryside', in N Holbrook and J Jurica (eds) 2006, *Twenty-Five Years of Archaeology in Gloucestershire: a review of discoveries and new thinking in Gloucestershire, South Gloucestershire and Bristol 1979–2004*, Bristol Gloucestershire Archaeol. Rep. **3**, Cirencester, Cotswold Archaeology, 167–87

Bryant, V. 2004 'Medieval and early post-medieval pottery', in H. Dalwood and R. Edwards, 2004 *Excavations at Deansway, Worcestershire 1988-89: Romano-British small town to late medieval city* CBA Res. Rep. **139**, York, Council for British Archaeology

Cappers, R.T.J., Bekker, R.M. and Jans, J.E.A. 2006 *Digital seed atlas of the Netherlands, Groningen Archaeological Studies 4* Eelde, Barkhuis Publishing (www.seedatlas.nl)

Chaplin, R.E. 1971 *The study of animal bones from archaeological sites* London, Seminar Press

Charity Commission 1826–7 'Parish of Kings Stanley: The Trust of Deacon's Close', in 'Reports from Commissioners: Charities in England and Wales: Counties of Gloucester, Lancaster, Middlesex; Southampton, Surrey; York', Session: 21 November 1826 to 2 July 1827, Vol. IX 71, London, House of Commons

Clarke, H. 1984 *The archaeology of medieval England* London, British Museum

Clark, J. 2004 *The medieval horse and its equipment, c. 1150–1450* London, Museum of London

Collingwood, R.G. and Wright, R.P. 1993 *The Roman Inscriptions of Britain II, Instrumentum Domesticum, Fascicule 5 Gloucester*, Alan Sutton

Cutler, D.F. and Gale, R. 2000 *Plants in archaeology, identification manual of artefacts of plant origin from Europe and the Mediterranean* Kew, Westbury Scientific

Dyer, C. 1988 'The consumption of freshwater fish in medieval England', in M. Aston (ed.) 1988, *Medieval fish, fisheries and fishponds in England* BAR Brit. Ser. **182** (i), Oxford, British Archaeological Reports, 27–38

Fock, J. 1966 *Metrische Untersuchungen an Metapodien einiger europäischer Rinderrassen* Unpublished dissertation, Munich, Universität München

Grant, A. 1988 'Food, status and religion in England in the middle ages: An archaeozoological perspective', in L. Bodson (ed.) 1988, *L'Animal dans L'Alimentation Humaine: Les Critères des Choix* Paris, L'Homme et l'Animal, Société de Recherche Interdisciplinaire, 139–46

Habermehl, K-H. 1975 *Die Altersbestimmung bei Haus- und Labortieren* Berlin, Verlag Paul Parey

Heighway, C. 1989 'Excavations near the site of St George's Church, Kings Stanley', *Glevensis* **23**, 33–42

Heighway, C. 2007 'Excavations at Kings Stanley 1961–1981: an account of excavations near St George's Church', unpublished report

Heller, I., Kienast, F., Schoch, W. and Schweingruber, F.H. 2004 *Wood anatomy of Central European species* (www.woodanatomy.ch)

Herbert, N.M. 1972 'Kings Stanley', in C.R. Elrington and N.M. Herbert (eds) 1972, *The Victoria History of the County of Gloucester, Vol. X* London, Oxford University Press, 242–56

Ireland, C.A. 1998 'The Pottery', in D. Wilkinson and A. McWhirr 1998, *Cirencester Anglo-Saxon Church and medieval Abbey* Cirencester Excavations **IV**, Cirencester, Cotswold Archaeological Trust, 98–140

Iregren, E. 2002 *Bildkompendium: Historisk osteologi* Dept Archaeol. Ancient Hist. Rep. Ser. **85**, Lund, University of Lund

May, E. 1985 'Widerristhöhe und Langknochenmaße bei Pferden – ein immer noch aktuelles Problem', *Zeitschrift für Säugetierkunde* **50**, 368–82

Radu, V. 2005 *Atlas for identification of bony fish bones from archaeological sites* Asociaţia Română de Arheologie Studii de Preistorie Supplementum **1**, Bucharest, Editura

Rogers, J. and Waldron, T. 1995 *A field guide to joint disease in archaeology* Chichester, John Wiley and Sons

Schmid, E. 1972 *Atlas of animal bones: For prehistorians, archaeologists and quaternary geologists* Amsterdam, Elsevier

Serjeantson, D. and Woolgar, C.M. 2006 'Fish consumption in medieval England', in C.M. Woolgar, D. Serjeantson and T. Waldron (eds.) 2006, 102–30

Silver, I.A. 1970 'The ageing of domestic animals', in D. Brothwell and E. Higgs (eds.) 1970, *Science in Archaeology: A survey of progress and research* New York, Praeger, 283–302

Stace, C. 1997 *New flora of the British Isles* Cambridge, Cambridge University Press

Steane, J.M. 1985 *The archaeology of medieval England and Wales* London, Croom Helm

Stone, D.J. 2006 'The consumption of field crops in late medieval England', in C.M. Woolgar, D. Serjeantson and T. Waldron (eds.) 2006, 11–26

Taylor, C. 1977 'Polyfocal Settlement and the English Village', *Medieval Archaeol.* **21**, 189–93

Tilley M., Douthwaite, A. and Devine, V. 2007 'Gloucestershire Historic Towns Survey: Stroud District Archaeological Assessments: Kings Stanley', unpublished Gloucestershire County Council report

Tomber, R. and Dore, J. 1998 *The National Roman Fabric Reference Collection: a handbook* London, Museum of London Archaeology Service

von den Driesch, A. 1976 *A guide to the measurement of animal bones from archaeological sites.* Peabody Museum Bulletins **1**, Cambridge, Harvard University.

Weiss Adamson, M. 2004 *Food in medieval times* Westport, Greenwood Press

Wheeler, E.A., Baas, P. and Gasson, P.E. 1989 'IAWA list of microscopic features for hardwood identification', *IAWA Bulletin* **10**, 219–332

Woolgar, C.M. 1999 *The great household in late medieval England* London, Yale University Press

Woolgar, C.M., Serjeantson, D. and Waldron, T. (eds) 2006 *Food in medieval England: diet and nutrition* Oxford, Oxford University Press